DEAR FUTURE EXAM SUCCESS STORY

First of all, **THANK YOU** for purchasing Mometrix study materials!

Second, congratulations! You are one of the few determined test-takers who are committed to doing whatever it takes to excel on your exam. **You have come to the right place.** We developed these study materials with one goal in mind: to deliver you the information you need in a format that's concise and easy to use.

In addition to optimizing your guide for the content of the test, we've outlined our recommended steps for breaking down the preparation process into small, attainable goals so you can make sure you stay on track.

We've also analyzed the entire test-taking process, identifying the most common pitfalls and showing how you can overcome them and be ready for any curveball the test throws you.

Standardized testing is one of the biggest obstacles on your road to success, which only increases the importance of doing well in the high-pressure, high-stakes environment of test day. Your results on this test could have a significant impact on your future, and this guide provides the information and practical advice to help you achieve your full potential on test day.

Your success is our success

We would love to hear from you! If you would like to share the story of your exam success or if you have any questions or comments in regard to our products, please contact us at **800-673-8175** or **support@mometrix.com**.

Thanks again for your business and we wish you continued success!

Sincerely,
The Mometrix Test Preparation Team

I0892269

Need more help? Check out our flashcards at:
http://MometrixFlashcards.com/TExES

Mometrix
TEST PREPARATION

TExES

AAFCS Hospitality, Nutrition, & Food Science 8-12 (201)

Secrets Study Guide

TABLE OF CONTENTS

INTRODUCTION — 1

SECRET KEY #1 – PLAN BIG, STUDY SMALL — 2

SECRET KEY #2 – MAKE YOUR STUDYING COUNT — 3

SECRET KEY #3 – PRACTICE THE RIGHT WAY — 4

SECRET KEY #4 – PACE YOURSELF — 6

SECRET KEY #5 – HAVE A PLAN FOR GUESSING — 7

TEST-TAKING STRATEGIES — 10

INTEGRATION OF FOUNDATIONS — 15
- CHAPTER QUIZ — 19

NUTRITION, WELLNESS, AND FOOD SCIENCES — 20
- NUTRITION AND WELLNESS — 20
- HEALTH AND WELLNESS — 29
- MEAL PLANNING AND SERVICE — 40
- CHAPTER QUIZ — 45

FOOD, LODGING, AND HOSPITALITY — 46
- CHAPTER QUIZ — 56

TExES PRACTICE TEST — 57
- INTEGRATION OF FOUNDATIONS — 57
- NUTRITION, WELLNESS, AND FOOD SERVICE — 59

ANSWER KEY AND EXPLANATIONS — 63
- INTEGRATION OF FOUNDATIONS — 63
- NUTRITION, WELLNESS, AND FOOD SERVICE — 65

HOW TO OVERCOME TEST ANXIETY — 68

ONLINE RESOURCES — 74

Introduction

Thank you for purchasing this resource! You have made the choice to prepare yourself for a test that could have a huge impact on your future, and this guide is designed to help you be fully ready for test day. Obviously, it's important to have a solid understanding of the test material, but you also need to be prepared for the unique environment and stressors of the test, so that you can perform to the best of your abilities.

For this purpose, the first section that appears in this guide is the **Secret Keys**. We've devoted countless hours to meticulously researching what works and what doesn't, and we've boiled down our findings to the five most impactful steps you can take to improve your performance on the test. We start at the beginning with study planning and move through the preparation process, all the way to the testing strategies that will help you get the most out of what you know when you're finally sitting in front of the test.

We recommend that you start preparing for your test as far in advance as possible. However, if you've bought this guide as a last-minute study resource and only have a few days before your test, we recommend that you skip over the first two Secret Keys since they address a long-term study plan.

If you struggle with **test anxiety**, we strongly encourage you to check out our recommendations for how you can overcome it. Test anxiety is a formidable foe, but it can be beaten, and we want to make sure you have the tools you need to defeat it.

Secret Key #1 – Plan Big, Study Small

There's a lot riding on your performance. If you want to ace this test, you're going to need to keep your skills sharp and the material fresh in your mind. You need a plan that lets you review everything you need to know while still fitting in your schedule. We'll break this strategy down into three categories.

Information Organization

Start with the information you already have: the official test outline. From this, you can make a complete list of all the concepts you need to cover before the test. Organize these concepts into groups that can be studied together, and create a list of any related vocabulary you need to learn so you can brush up on any difficult terms. You'll want to keep this vocabulary list handy once you actually start studying since you may need to add to it along the way.

Time Management

Once you have your set of study concepts, decide how to spread them out over the time you have left before the test. Break your study plan into small, clear goals so you have a manageable task for each day and know exactly what you're doing. Then just focus on one small step at a time. When you manage your time this way, you don't need to spend hours at a time studying. Studying a small block of content for a short period each day helps you retain information better and avoid stressing over how much you have left to do. You can relax knowing that you have a plan to cover everything in time. In order for this strategy to be effective though, you have to start studying early and stick to your schedule. Avoid the exhaustion and futility that comes from last-minute cramming!

Study Environment

The environment you study in has a big impact on your learning. Studying in a coffee shop, while probably more enjoyable, is not likely to be as fruitful as studying in a quiet room. It's important to keep distractions to a minimum. You're only planning to study for a short block of time, so make the most of it. Don't pause to check your phone or get up to find a snack. It's also important to **avoid multitasking**. Research has consistently shown that multitasking will make your studying dramatically less effective. Your study area should also be comfortable and well-lit so you don't have the distraction of straining your eyes or sitting on an uncomfortable chair.

The time of day you study is also important. You want to be rested and alert. Don't wait until just before bedtime. Study when you'll be most likely to comprehend and remember. Even better, if you know what time of day your test will be, set that time aside for study. That way your brain will be used to working on that subject at that specific time and you'll have a better chance of recalling information.

Finally, it can be helpful to team up with others who are studying for the same test. Your actual studying should be done in as isolated an environment as possible, but the work of organizing the information and setting up the study plan can be divided up. In between study sessions, you can discuss with your teammates the concepts that you're all studying and quiz each other on the details. Just be sure that your teammates are as serious about the test as you are. If you find that your study time is being replaced with social time, you might need to find a new team.

Secret Key #2 – Make Your Studying Count

You're devoting a lot of time and effort to preparing for this test, so you want to be absolutely certain it will pay off. This means doing more than just reading the content and hoping you can remember it on test day. It's important to make every minute of study count. There are two main areas you can focus on to make your studying count.

Retention

It doesn't matter how much time you study if you can't remember the material. You need to make sure you are retaining the concepts. To check your retention of the information you're learning, try recalling it at later times with minimal prompting. Try carrying around flashcards and glance at one or two from time to time or ask a friend who's also studying for the test to quiz you.

To enhance your retention, look for ways to put the information into practice so that you can apply it rather than simply recalling it. If you're using the information in practical ways, it will be much easier to remember. Similarly, it helps to solidify a concept in your mind if you're not only reading it to yourself but also explaining it to someone else. Ask a friend to let you teach them about a concept you're a little shaky on (or speak aloud to an imaginary audience if necessary). As you try to summarize, define, give examples, and answer your friend's questions, you'll understand the concepts better and they will stay with you longer. Finally, step back for a big picture view and ask yourself how each piece of information fits with the whole subject. When you link the different concepts together and see them working together as a whole, it's easier to remember the individual components.

Finally, practice showing your work on any multi-step problems, even if you're just studying. Writing out each step you take to solve a problem will help solidify the process in your mind, and you'll be more likely to remember it during the test.

Modality

Modality simply refers to the means or method by which you study. Choosing a study modality that fits your own individual learning style is crucial. No two people learn best in exactly the same way, so it's important to know your strengths and use them to your advantage.

For example, if you learn best by visualization, focus on visualizing a concept in your mind and draw an image or a diagram. Try color-coding your notes, illustrating them, or creating symbols that will trigger your mind to recall a learned concept. If you learn best by hearing or discussing information, find a study partner who learns the same way or read aloud to yourself. Think about how to put the information in your own words. Imagine that you are giving a lecture on the topic and record yourself so you can listen to it later.

For any learning style, flashcards can be helpful. Organize the information so you can take advantage of spare moments to review. Underline key words or phrases. Use different colors for different categories. Mnemonic devices (such as creating a short list in which every item starts with the same letter) can also help with retention. Find what works best for you and use it to store the information in your mind most effectively and easily.

Secret Key #3 – Practice the Right Way

Your success on test day depends not only on how many hours you put into preparing, but also on whether you prepared the right way. It's good to check along the way to see if your studying is paying off. One of the most effective ways to do this is by taking practice tests to evaluate your progress. Practice tests are useful because they show exactly where you need to improve. Every time you take a practice test, pay special attention to these three groups of questions:

- The questions you got wrong
- The questions you had to guess on, even if you guessed right
- The questions you found difficult or slow to work through

This will show you exactly what your weak areas are, and where you need to devote more study time. Ask yourself why each of these questions gave you trouble. Was it because you didn't understand the material? Was it because you didn't remember the vocabulary? Do you need more repetitions on this type of question to build speed and confidence? Dig into those questions and figure out how you can strengthen your weak areas as you go back to review the material.

Additionally, many practice tests have a section explaining the answer choices. It can be tempting to read the explanation and think that you now have a good understanding of the concept. However, an explanation likely only covers part of the question's broader context. Even if the explanation makes perfect sense, **go back and investigate** every concept related to the question until you're positive you have a thorough understanding.

As you go along, keep in mind that the practice test is just that: practice. Memorizing these questions and answers will not be very helpful on the actual test because it is unlikely to have any of the same exact questions. If you only know the right answers to the sample questions, you won't be prepared for the real thing. **Study the concepts** until you understand them fully, and then you'll be able to answer any question that shows up on the test.

It's important to wait on the practice tests until you're ready. If you take a test on your first day of study, you may be overwhelmed by the amount of material covered and how much you need to learn. Work up to it gradually.

On test day, you'll need to be prepared for answering questions, managing your time, and using the test-taking strategies you've learned. It's a lot to balance, like a mental marathon that will have a big impact on your future. Like training for a marathon, you'll need to start slowly and work your way up. When test day arrives, you'll be ready.

Start with the strategies you've read in the first two Secret Keys—plan your course and study in the way that works best for you. If you have time, consider using multiple study resources to get different approaches to the same concepts. It can be helpful to see difficult concepts from more than one angle. Then find a good source for practice tests. Many times, the test website will suggest potential study resources or provide sample tests.

Practice Test Strategy

If you're able to find at least three practice tests, we recommend this strategy:

Untimed and Open-Book Practice

Take the first test with no time constraints and with your notes and study guide handy. Take your time and focus on applying the strategies you've learned.

Timed and Open-Book Practice

Take the second practice test open-book as well, but set a timer and practice pacing yourself to finish in time.

Timed and Closed-Book Practice

Take any other practice tests as if it were test day. Set a timer and put away your study materials. Sit at a table or desk in a quiet room, imagine yourself at the testing center, and answer questions as quickly and accurately as possible.

Keep repeating timed and closed-book tests on a regular basis until you run out of practice tests or it's time for the actual test. Your mind will be ready for the schedule and stress of test day, and you'll be able to focus on recalling the material you've learned.

Secret Key #4 – Pace Yourself

Once you're fully prepared for the material on the test, your biggest challenge on test day will be managing your time. Just knowing that the clock is ticking can make you panic even if you have plenty of time left. Work on pacing yourself so you can build confidence against the time constraints of the exam. Pacing is a difficult skill to master, especially in a high-pressure environment, so **practice is vital**.

Set time expectations for your pace based on how much time is available. For example, if a section has 60 questions and the time limit is 30 minutes, you know you have to average 30 seconds or less per question in order to answer them all. Although 30 seconds is the hard limit, set 25 seconds per question as your goal, so you reserve extra time to spend on harder questions. When you budget extra time for the harder questions, you no longer have any reason to stress when those questions take longer to answer.

Don't let this time expectation distract you from working through the test at a calm, steady pace, but keep it in mind so you don't spend too much time on any one question. Recognize that taking extra time on one question you don't understand may keep you from answering two that you do understand later in the test. If your time limit for a question is up and you're still not sure of the answer, mark it and move on, and come back to it later if the time and the test format allow. If the testing format doesn't allow you to return to earlier questions, just make an educated guess; then put it out of your mind and move on.

On the easier questions, be careful not to rush. It may seem wise to hurry through them so you have more time for the challenging ones, but it's not worth missing one if you know the concept and just didn't take the time to read the question fully. Work efficiently but make sure you understand the question and have looked at all of the answer choices, since more than one may seem right at first.

Even if you're paying attention to the time, you may find yourself a little behind at some point. You should speed up to get back on track, but do so wisely. Don't panic; just take a few seconds less on each question until you're caught up. Don't guess without thinking, but do look through the answer choices and eliminate any you know are wrong. If you can get down to two choices, it is often worthwhile to guess from those. Once you've chosen an answer, move on and don't dwell on any that you skipped or had to hurry through. If a question was taking too long, chances are it was one of the harder ones, so you weren't as likely to get it right anyway.

On the other hand, if you find yourself getting ahead of schedule, it may be beneficial to slow down a little. The more quickly you work, the more likely you are to make a careless mistake that will affect your score. You've budgeted time for each question, so don't be afraid to spend that time. Practice an efficient but careful pace to get the most out of the time you have.

Secret Key #5 – Have a Plan for Guessing

When you're taking the test, you may find yourself stuck on a question. Some of the answer choices seem better than others, but you don't see the one answer choice that is obviously correct. What do you do?

The scenario described above is very common, yet most test takers have not effectively prepared for it. Developing and practicing a plan for guessing may be one of the single most effective uses of your time as you get ready for the exam.

In developing your plan for guessing, there are three questions to address:

- When should you start the guessing process?
- How should you narrow down the choices?
- Which answer should you choose?

When to Start the Guessing Process

Unless your plan for guessing is to select C every time (which, despite its merits, is not what we recommend), you need to leave yourself enough time to apply your answer elimination strategies. Since you have a limited amount of time for each question, that means that if you're going to give yourself the best shot at guessing correctly, you have to decide quickly whether or not you will guess.

Of course, the best-case scenario is that you don't have to guess at all, so first, see if you can answer the question based on your knowledge of the subject and basic reasoning skills. Focus on the key words in the question and try to jog your memory of related topics. Give yourself a chance to bring the knowledge to mind, but once you realize that you don't have (or you can't access) the knowledge you need to answer the question, it's time to start the guessing process.

It's almost always better to start the guessing process too early than too late. It only takes a few seconds to remember something and answer the question from knowledge. Carefully eliminating wrong answer choices takes longer. Plus, going through the process of eliminating answer choices can actually help jog your memory.

Summary: Start the guessing process as soon as you decide that you can't answer the question based on your knowledge.

How to Narrow Down the Choices

The next chapter in this book (**Test-Taking Strategies**) includes a wide range of strategies for how to approach questions and how to look for answer choices to eliminate. You will definitely want to read those carefully, practice them, and figure out which ones work best for you. Here though, we're going to address a mindset rather than a particular strategy.

Your odds of guessing an answer correctly depend on how many options you are choosing from.

Number of options left	5	4	3	2	1
Odds of guessing correctly	20%	25%	33%	50%	100%

You can see from this chart just how valuable it is to be able to eliminate incorrect answers and make an educated guess, but there are two things that many test takers do that cause them to miss out on the benefits of guessing:

- Accidentally eliminating the correct answer
- Selecting an answer based on an impression

We'll look at the first one here, and the second one in the next section.

To avoid accidentally eliminating the correct answer, we recommend a thought exercise called **the $5 challenge**. In this challenge, you only eliminate an answer choice from contention if you are willing to bet $5 on it being wrong. Why $5? Five dollars is a small but not insignificant amount of money. It's an amount you could afford to lose but wouldn't want to throw away. And while losing $5 once might not hurt too much, doing it twenty times will set you back $100. In the same way, each small decision you make—eliminating a choice here, guessing on a question there—won't by itself impact your score very much, but when you put them all together, they can make a big difference. By holding each answer choice elimination decision to a higher standard, you can reduce the risk of accidentally eliminating the correct answer.

The $5 challenge can also be applied in a positive sense: If you are willing to bet $5 that an answer choice *is* correct, go ahead and mark it as correct.

Summary: Only eliminate an answer choice if you are willing to bet $5 that it is wrong.

Which Answer to Choose

You're taking the test. You've run into a hard question and decided you'll have to guess. You've eliminated all the answer choices you're willing to bet $5 on. Now you have to pick an answer. Why do we even need to talk about this? Why can't you just pick whichever one you feel like when the time comes?

The answer to these questions is that if you don't come into the test with a plan, you'll rely on your impression to select an answer choice, and if you do that, you risk falling into a trap. The test writers know that everyone who takes their test will be guessing on some of the questions, so they intentionally write wrong answer choices to seem plausible. You still have to pick an answer though, and if the wrong answer choices are designed to look right, how can you ever be sure that you're not falling for their trap? The best solution we've found to this dilemma is to take the decision out of your hands entirely. Here is the process we recommend:

Once you've eliminated any choices that you are confident (willing to bet $5) are wrong, select the first remaining choice as your answer.

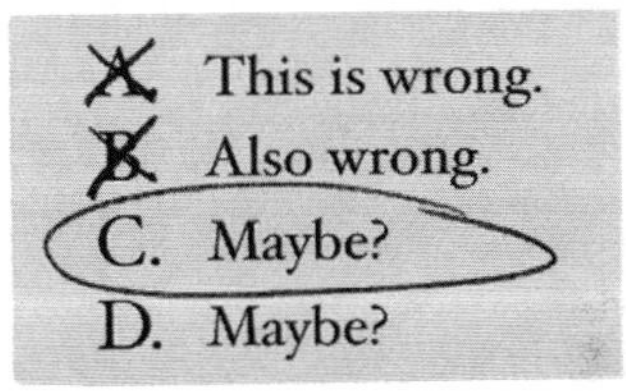

Whether you choose to select the first remaining choice, the second, or the last, the important thing is that you use some preselected standard. Using this approach guarantees that you will not be enticed into selecting an answer choice that looks right, because you are not basing your decision on how the answer choices look.

This is not meant to make you question your knowledge. Instead, it is to help you recognize the difference between your knowledge and your impressions. There's a huge difference between thinking an answer is right because of what you know, and thinking an answer is right because it looks or sounds like it should be right.

Summary: To ensure that your selection is appropriately random, make a predetermined selection from among all answer choices you have not eliminated.

Test-Taking Strategies

This section contains a list of test-taking strategies that you may find helpful as you work through the test. By taking what you know and applying logical thought, you can maximize your chances of answering any question correctly!

It is very important to realize that every question is different and every person is different: no single strategy will work on every question, and no single strategy will work for every person. That's why we've included all of them here, so you can try them out and determine which ones work best for different types of questions and which ones work best for you.

Question Strategies

✓ Read Carefully

Read the question and the answer choices carefully. Don't miss the question because you misread the terms. You have plenty of time to read each question thoroughly and make sure you understand what is being asked. Yet a happy medium must be attained, so don't waste too much time. You must read carefully and efficiently.

✓ Contextual Clues

Look for contextual clues. If the question includes a word you are not familiar with, look at the immediate context for some indication of what the word might mean. Contextual clues can often give you all the information you need to decipher the meaning of an unfamiliar word. Even if you can't determine the meaning, you may be able to narrow down the possibilities enough to make a solid guess at the answer to the question.

✓ Prefixes

If you're having trouble with a word in the question or answer choices, try dissecting it. Take advantage of every clue that the word might include. Prefixes can be a huge help. Usually, they allow you to determine a basic meaning. *Pre-* means before, *post-* means after, *pro-* is positive, *de-* is negative. From prefixes, you can get an idea of the general meaning of the word and try to put it into context.

✓ Hedge Words

Watch out for critical hedge words, such as *likely, may, can, often, almost, mostly, usually, generally, rarely,* and *sometimes.* Question writers insert these hedge phrases to cover every possibility. Often an answer choice will be wrong simply because it leaves no room for exception. Be on guard for answer choices that have definitive words such as *exactly* and *always.*

✓ Switchback Words

Stay alert for *switchbacks.* These are the words and phrases frequently used to alert you to shifts in thought. The most common switchback words are *but, although,* and *however.* Others include *nevertheless, on the other hand, even though, while, in spite of, despite,* and *regardless of.* Switchback words are important to catch because they can change the direction of the question or an answer choice.

✓ Face Value

When in doubt, use common sense. Accept the situation in the problem at face value. Don't read too much into it. These problems will not require you to make wild assumptions. If you have to go beyond creativity and warp time or space in order to have an answer choice fit the question, then you should move on and consider the other answer choices. These are normal problems rooted in reality. The applicable relationship or explanation may not be readily apparent, but it is there for you to figure out. Use your common sense to interpret anything that isn't clear.

Answer Choice Strategies

✓ Answer Selection

The most thorough way to pick an answer choice is to identify and eliminate wrong answers until only one is left, then confirm it is the correct answer. Sometimes an answer choice may immediately seem right, but be careful. The test writers will usually put more than one reasonable answer choice on each question, so take a second to read all of them and make sure that the other choices are not equally obvious. As long as you have time left, it is better to read every answer choice than to pick the first one that looks right without checking the others.

✓ Answer Choice Families

An answer choice family consists of two (in rare cases, three) answer choices that are very similar in construction and cannot all be true at the same time. If you see two answer choices that are direct opposites or parallels, one of them is usually the correct answer. For instance, if one answer choice says that quantity *x* increases and another either says that quantity *x* decreases (opposite) or says that quantity *y* increases (parallel), then those answer choices would fall into the same family. An answer choice that doesn't match the construction of the answer choice family is more likely to be incorrect. Most questions will not have answer choice families, but when they do appear, you should be prepared to recognize them.

✓ Eliminate Answers

Eliminate answer choices as soon as you realize they are wrong, but make sure you consider all possibilities. If you are eliminating answer choices and realize that the last one you are left with is also wrong, don't panic. Start over and consider each choice again. There may be something you missed the first time that you will realize on the second pass.

✓ Avoid Fact Traps

Don't be distracted by an answer choice that is factually true but doesn't answer the question. You are looking for the choice that answers the question. Stay focused on what the question is asking for so you don't accidentally pick an answer that is true but incorrect. Always go back to the question and make sure the answer choice you've selected actually answers the question and is not merely a true statement.

✓ Extreme Statements

In general, you should avoid answers that put forth extreme actions as standard practice or proclaim controversial ideas as established fact. An answer choice that states the "process should be used in certain situations, if…" is much more likely to be correct than one that states the "process should be discontinued completely." The first is a calm rational statement and doesn't even make a definitive, uncompromising stance, using a hedge word *if* to provide wiggle room, whereas the second choice is far more extreme.

✓ Benchmark

As you read through the answer choices and you come across one that seems to answer the question well, mentally select that answer choice. This is not your final answer, but it's the one that will help you evaluate the other answer choices. The one that you selected is your benchmark or standard for judging each of the other answer choices. Every other answer choice must be compared to your benchmark. That choice is correct until proven otherwise by another answer choice beating it. If you find a better answer, then that one becomes your new benchmark. Once you've decided that no other choice answers the question as well as your benchmark, you have your final answer.

✓ Predict the Answer

Before you even start looking at the answer choices, it is often best to try to predict the answer. When you come up with the answer on your own, it is easier to avoid distractions and traps because you will know exactly what to look for. The right answer choice is unlikely to be word-for-word what you came up with, but it should be a close match. Even if you are confident that you have the right answer, you should still take the time to read each option before moving on.

General Strategies

✓ Tough Questions

If you are stumped on a problem or it appears too hard or too difficult, don't waste time. Move on! Remember though, if you can quickly check for obviously incorrect answer choices, your chances of guessing correctly are greatly improved. Before you completely give up, at least try to knock out a couple of possible answers. Eliminate what you can and then guess at the remaining answer choices before moving on.

✓ Check Your Work

Since you will probably not know every term listed and the answer to every question, it is important that you get credit for the ones that you do know. Don't miss any questions through careless mistakes. If at all possible, try to take a second to look back over your answer selection and make sure you've selected the correct answer choice and haven't made a costly careless mistake (such as marking an answer choice that you didn't mean to mark). This quick double check should more than pay for itself in caught mistakes for the time it costs.

✓ Pace Yourself

It's easy to be overwhelmed when you're looking at a page full of questions; your mind is confused and full of random thoughts, and the clock is ticking down faster than you would like. Calm down and maintain the pace that you have set for yourself. Especially as you get down to the last few minutes of the test, don't let the small numbers on the clock make you panic. As long as you are on track by monitoring your pace, you are guaranteed to have time for each question.

✓ Don't Rush

It is very easy to make errors when you are in a hurry. Maintaining a fast pace in answering questions is pointless if it makes you miss questions that you would have gotten right otherwise. Test writers like to include distracting information and wrong answers that seem right. Taking a little extra time to avoid careless mistakes can make all the difference in your test score. Find a pace that allows you to be confident in the answers that you select.

⊘ KEEP MOVING

Panicking will not help you pass the test, so do your best to stay calm and keep moving. Taking deep breaths and going through the answer elimination steps you practiced can help to break through a stress barrier and keep your pace.

Final Notes

The combination of a solid foundation of content knowledge and the confidence that comes from practicing your plan for applying that knowledge is the key to maximizing your performance on test day. As your foundation of content knowledge is built up and strengthened, you'll find that the strategies included in this chapter become more and more effective in helping you quickly sift through the distractions and traps of the test to isolate the correct answer.

Now that you're preparing to move forward into the test content chapters of this book, be sure to keep your goal in mind. As you read, think about how you will be able to apply this information on the test. If you've already seen sample questions for the test and you have an idea of the question format and style, try to come up with questions of your own that you can answer based on what you're reading. This will give you valuable practice applying your knowledge in the same ways you can expect to on test day.

Good luck and good studying!

Integration of Foundations

Careers

Family and consumer science skills are useful in food management, financial management, human resources, public relations, tailoring, dress-making, etc. Indeed, regardless of career, an individual always finds a use for these skills in life. An individual in food management needs to know about nutrition and the proper handling and preparation of food. Financial advisors need to know how to assess resources, cut costs, and determine how much an individual needs to save before retirement. Human resource and public relations managers need social skills and training in time and resource management, human development, and psychology. Finally, tailors and dressmakers use their knowledge of textiles and textile design to create better garments.

In order to help students determine their interests and develop their skills, teachers should give them some example descriptions of various careers. Some of these examples may be family and consumer science careers, though it is not necessary for them all to be so. The class should examine a diverse sampling of different careers, especially since family and consumer science skills can be applied to virtually any setting. For example, a construction worker might not need to know about food, textiles, or housing design, but they still need to know various problem-solving techniques. It can also be extremely useful for students to get some hands-on experience applying family and consumer science concepts to the tasks associated with different careers.

Family and Consumer Education

Family and consumer education aims to improve a variety of skills that are essential for the day-to-day functioning of an individual and their family. Family and consumer education includes specific topics such as family interaction, human development, nutrition, consumer economics, types of housing and housing design, textiles, parenting, and the appropriate cooking and handling of foods. Family and consumer education covers both the physical and the psychological needs of the individual, and emphasizes appropriate social interaction between the individual and the rest of society.

Work Simplification

Work simplification is the process of discovering and implementing a series of procedures allowing an individual or a group of individuals to complete a task more easily and efficiently. Based on the particular type of task being performed, work can be simplified in a number of ways by determining the best possible way to complete a task without significantly impacting the overall quality of the work. Some of the basic methods used to make any task easier and more efficient include ensuring that individuals have access to necessary equipment, that work areas are organized, and that any steps in the work process that do not directly affect the outcome of the work are eliminated.

Goals of Family and Consumer Sciences Education

The Association for Career and Technical Education has identified nine goals commonly associated with family and consumer sciences education. These nine goals include:

1. Improving the overall quality of life for individuals and families
2. Helping individuals and families become responsible members of society
3. Encouraging healthy eating habits, nutrition, and lifestyles
4. Improving how individuals and families manage their resources

5. Helping individuals and families balance their personal, family, and work lives
6. Teaching individuals better problem-solving techniques
7. Encouraging personal and career development
8. Teaching individuals to successfully function as both consumers and providers
9. Recognizing human worth and taking responsibility for one's own actions

The first of the nine goals established for family and consumer sciences education is to improve the overall quality of life for individuals and families, which is also the primary mission of all the goals. Family and consumer sciences education teaches people about how individuals, families, and the rest of society interact with each other, along with methods for improving those interactions. These methods include problem-solving techniques, common scams and problems to avoid, methods to stay healthy both physically and psychologically, and the distribution of a variety of other information regarding how the individual, family, and the rest of society function. Ultimately, family and consumer sciences education strives to improve the quality of life by educating individuals and families in the best manner to function on a day-to-day basis. However, this goal is truly accomplished only when the other eight goals of family and consumer sciences education are met as well.

Basic Concepts of Family and Consumer Education

There are several concepts at the core of family and consumer education, but one of the most important concepts is that families form the basic unit of society. Another important concept of family and consumer education is that individuals need to be life-long learners in order to develop and function successfully. Finally, family and consumer education promotes the idea that individuals and families need to have an understanding of the advantages of experimenting with different decision-making methods and diverse ways of thinking in order to solve any given problem.

Occupational Family and Consumer Sciences Education

Occupational family and consumer sciences education is a teaching discipline that is similar to the standard discipline of family and consumer education but focuses less on the skills for day-to-day living and more on how those skills can be used in the workplace. Occupational family and consumer sciences education covers information regarding skills that can commonly be applied in fields such as health services, food service, child care, hospitality, fashion design, interior design, and many other similar fields. Occupational family and consumer sciences education places more emphasis on family and consumer skills that directly relate to a career, such as management techniques and ethical businesses practices, than the standard family and consumer education discipline. The occupational family and consumer sciences education discipline ultimately takes the skills that an individual has learned from the standard discipline and shows how those skills can be applied to a career.

Community Advisory Committees

Community advisory committees can be extremely useful to an education professional who is attempting to determine what areas of the family and consumer science discipline a teaching plan should emphasize because the committees offer insight into the concerns and demographics of the students. Each community has its own problems, concerns, and level of diversity, and it is important that a family and consumer science teacher can recognize and focus on areas of concern in the school's community. For example, a community that is having problems with widespread teenage drug abuse and teenage suicide may want the community's family and consumer science teachers to focus more on the topics of avoiding substance abuse and handling depression. The goal of a family and consumer sciences educator is to improve the overall quality of life for the students and their families, and the educator cannot do that if they do not know what problems need to be addressed.

Some of the functions that community advisory committees perform, other than offering advice to education professionals, include assessing the performance of family and consumer science programs; assessing the performance of students with special needs; and providing equipment, technology, and resources for family and consumer science programs. These resources may include raw materials, textile samples, charts and diagrams, library books, and access to computers and design software. Community advisory committees also help students improve their chances of finding better jobs and careers and act as a public relations liaisons for local family and consumer science programs. Ultimately, the primary purpose of a family and consumer sciences community advisory committee is to ensure that a family and consumer sciences program has all of the resources and training necessary to achieve the program's goals.

LABORATORY SETTINGS

A **laboratory setting** is important for a family and consumer sciences educator because it offers students an opportunity to gain hands-on experience using a variety of skills and techniques. Many important areas of the family and consumer sciences discipline center around using a combination of various skills to achieve a certain end result, and sometimes the best way to teach the appropriate way to integrate these skills is through experience. A laboratory setting offers students a place to demonstrate and improve their skills related to the family and consumer science field with the advantage of having a teacher present to answer questions and correct mistakes. Some examples of useful laboratory settings for the family and consumer sciences field include kitchens or food science laboratories, day care centers, and testing laboratories for textiles and consumer products.

DEMONSTRATING FAMILY AND CONSUMER SCIENCE CONCEPTS

There are a large number of methods that an educator can use to demonstrate concepts related to family and consumer sciences, but the best methods always involve promoting students' active participation. Some examples of active participation include allowing students to use a sewing machine; having students test the qualities of various textiles to see how soft, lustrous, resilient, absorbent, etc. each material is; and requiring students to prepare a meal. Students can also demonstrate active participation with the following activities: comparing advertisements to find the best offer for a particular product, examining common marketing tactics, visiting or working in a local daycare center, and being involved in local community service activities. Many of these activities serve not only as effective ways of teaching students about the important concepts of family and consumer sciences, but also as a means of testing the students' ability to apply the techniques, skills, and information that they have learned.

Usually, the best method an educator can use to verify whether a student understands a particular concept is to see if the student can actively apply the information they have learned to such everyday tasks as cooking, sewing, and time management; however, a student may not be able to demonstrate their understanding of certain concepts if a laboratory setting is not available. Alternative methods by which an educator can evaluate a student's level of comprehension include administering written tests, assigning projects and research papers, teaching students to design charts and diagrams, involving students in the evaluation of case studies and scenarios, and requiring students to keep a journal of their activities and eating habits. Which evaluation method an educator should use depends primarily on the curriculum being covered and the abilities of the students who are taking the class.

Professional Organizations

Professional organizations such as the American Association of Family and Consumer Sciences, also known as the AAFCS, play an important role in influencing the education of individuals in the methodology and knowledge associated with family and consumer sciences. Many of these local and national professional organizations offer seminars, courses, and publications on a wide range of topics directly to individuals and families to teach them about essential career and management skills, how to be smart consumers, the importance of following nutritional guidelines, and information about a wide range of other topics. These professional organizations also provide publications, advice, and curriculum guides to educational professionals that help these professionals teach and stay informed regarding important changes to the curriculum that result from changes in legislation, society, and the education system itself. These organizations also have a profound effect on family and consumer science education by influencing public policy and gathering support for programs that help educate and protect individuals and families from unsafe habits, business practices, products, and lifestyles.

FCCLA

The **FCCLA**, which stands for the **Family, Career, and Community Leaders of America**, is a youth organization for students in family and consumer science education. The FCCLA offers a variety of publications and programs designed to educate people about parenting, relationships, substance abuse, teen pregnancy, and teen violence, among other concerns. By focusing public attention to the problems that young people face, the FCCLA gains support for programs and laws that help protect young people and their families. The FCCLA also shows students how they can improve their family and consumer science skills and apply those skills later in life.

The FCCLA and other similar youth organizations play an important role in influencing national policy related to protecting families and consumers. Additionally, these organizations are important because they support family and consumer science educational programs, which strive to improve the overall quality of life for individuals and families by teaching people skills that will enable them to live better lives.

New Acts of Legislation

When a new act of legislation is passed, it can often have a profound impact on the types of materials used in family and consumer sciences classrooms, as well as the issues that should be addressed by family and consumer sciences education. It is important that individuals understand the legal protections and rights granted to them by the various acts put into place by state and federal governments. Since laws are constantly changing, family and consumer science educators must be able to adapt quickly and add information regarding new legislation to their curriculum.

Balancing Home and Work Roles

It is important that an individual can balance their work and home roles because it is becoming more and more common for individuals to have to act as both caregiver and provider for the family. The increasingly common presence of dual roles in society can be extremely difficult for an individual to balance, as there may be instances where work-related responsibilities and family-related responsibilities conflict with one another. Family and consumer sciences education attempts to teach individuals how to avoid and handle these conflicts through the use of successful life management tactics such as time and resources management, problem-solving and decision-making techniques, and effective communication techniques. Family and consumer sciences education also attempts to give individuals a basic understanding of what responsibilities and qualities are necessary for the successful completion of each role so that individuals can set better priorities and find better ways to plan their lives.

Chapter Quiz

Ready to see how well you retained what you just read? Scan the QR code to go directly to the chapter quiz interface for this study guide. If you're using a computer, simply visit the online resources page at **mometrix.com/resources719/texesfcshnds** and click the Chapter Quizzes link.

Nutrition, Wellness, and Food Sciences

Nutrition and Wellness

Preventing Anorexia, Bulimia, and Obesity

Unfortunately, there is no known way of completely eliminating the risk of an individual developing an eating-related condition such as **anorexia**, **bulimia**, and **obesity**, but it has been shown that some methods may significantly lower the risk of developing these conditions. The best way to reduce the risk of developing eating disorders or becoming obese is for parents to interact more with their children and make sure that they are teaching them good eating habits early on. It is also important that parents attempt to build-up the self-esteem of their children through interactions that show high esteem in both the parents and child. Children who have been taught good eating habits by their parents and who have been taught to have high self-esteem have been shown to eat more carefully, and therefore are at a significantly lower risk of becoming obese or developing eating disorders such as anorexia and bulimia.

Anorexia is an eating disorder in which an individual views their own body as being overweight, even though they are not, which causes the person to have an extreme, unfounded fear of gaining additional weight. This fear can lead individuals to use desperate and unhealthy methods to reduce their weight below what would normally be healthy. These methods include deliberate vomiting, limiting their food intake, exercising excessively without eating enough food, and using medications to flush their system. Anorexia is commonly found to affect young women, specifically during adolescence. It can pose a serious risk to an individual's health as the obsessive attempts to reduce body weight can affect the health of the heart, brain, immune system, muscles, and other organs. Anorexia can be extremely difficult to treat as it is a complicated psychological condition, but it has been shown that psychotherapy may be able to help the individual overcome the inaccurate perceptions she or he has regarding their own body.

Bulimia is an eating disorder, similar to anorexia, in which an individual views their own body as being unattractive or overweight, but lacks the ability to control their own eating. Bulimic individuals regularly eat an unhealthily large amount of food and then attempt to flush their systems to prevent themselves from gaining additional weight. Some of the methods individuals suffering from bulimia might use to flush food from their systems include deliberate vomiting, excessive exercise, and using diet pills, laxatives, ipecac, and other medications. Bulimia is most commonly found in women, especially younger women from ages 12 to 19, and can have a significant impact on the health of the individual. It can cause problems such as anemia, weakness, muscle and heart problems, dehydration, malnutrition, damage to the stomach, and a wide range of other problems. Bulimia is difficult to treat, but a combination of group psychotherapy and low doses of anti-psychotic medications have been shown to help.

Anorexia and bulimia are very similar disorders, but the one major difference between the two conditions is control. An individual suffering from anorexia is usually already below a healthy weight, still perceives that their own weight is unacceptable, and therefore attempts to lower that weight further by limiting food intake. Bulimic individuals, on the other hand, have no sense of control over their eating habits. They instead eat excessively and then attempt to overcompensate for their excessive food intake. In short, individuals suffering from anorexia are usually below what would normally be considered a healthy weight for their age and size and attempt to control their eating to reduce their weight further. Bulimic individuals, however, are usually above a healthy weight as they have no control over their own eating.

Obesity is a condition of the body where the individual has increased their own body weight significantly beyond what is normally considered healthy, usually by excessive eating. Obesity occurs because the individual takes in more food than their body can actually use, and the excess food is stored as fat. Overeating is the primary cause of obesity, but obesity can also be tied to family history, genetic factors, stress and lack of sleep, various illnesses and conditions, and many other causes. An individual who is obese is at a significantly higher risk for certain health problems, including problems with the heart, stomach, muscles, lungs, skin, nervous system, and many other areas of the body. The best way to treat obesity is through a well-balanced diet that eliminates excessive food intake and a rigorous exercise program. In extreme cases, individuals may also use medication or even surgery to help lower their weight.

Diabetes

Diabetes is a disease that prevents the body from producing or using a hormone called insulin, which the body needs to process sugar and use it as energy for the cells of the body. Since an individual with diabetes cannot produce insulin or cannot use what is produced, the body is unable to appropriately use the sugar that the cells need to survive. Instead the sugar builds up in the body, leading to a high sugar concentration in the blood, which is a condition known as hyperglycemia. Diabetes can lead to a series of dangerous health problems including the potential failure of the heart, kidneys, nerves, and eyes as well as conditions such as high blood pressure, blindness, poor healing of wounds, and many other dangerous conditions. There is currently no cure for diabetes, but the negative effects of diabetes can be controlled through careful monitoring of blood sugar levels, the use of a specific diet to maintain the individual's blood sugar, and through the use of certain drugs and/or insulin shots.

The three types of diabetes are **type 1**, **type 2**, and **gestational diabetes**. Type 1 diabetes is a form of diabetes in which the individual's own immune system mistakes the beta cells of the pancreas, which are the cells responsible for producing insulin, as being harmful and therefore attacks and destroys them. Type 1 diabetes prevents the individual from actually producing insulin. It is treated primarily through the use of a carefully constructed diet and insulin injections or the use of an insulin pump. Both type 2 diabetes and gestational diabetes are conditions in which the individual is either unable to produce enough insulin for the body or the cells of the body are unable to use the insulin correctly. Type 2 and gestational diabetes can both be treated through the use of a carefully monitored diet along with medication to help the body use the insulin appropriately. The only major difference between type 2 diabetes and gestational diabetes is that gestational diabetes occurs specifically due to hormones present during pregnancy.

There is currently no way to completely prevent an individual from developing diabetes, but the risk of developing certain forms of diabetes can be reduced. The risk of type 2 diabetes and gestational diabetes can be reduced by eating a more healthy diet high in fiber and whole grains, exercising regularly, and lowering the amount of high-fat foods that the individual eats. It has also been suggested that the risk of a mother developing gestational diabetes may be reduced through breast-feeding as it allows the mother to release some of the excess hormones present in her body as a result of the pregnancy. The risk of type 2 and gestational diabetes can be reduced, but there is, unfortunately, no known way of preventing type 1 diabetes, as researchers know very little about the exact causes of the disease.

Review Video: Diabetes Mellitus
Visit mometrix.com/academy and enter code: 501396

Hypertension

Hypertension is a condition in which an individual's blood pressure is regularly higher than the range that is normally acceptable. The blood pressure of a healthy individual should be somewhere between 90/50 and 120/80, and anything over 140/90 is considered to be a high blood pressure. Anything between 120/80 and 140/90 is considered to be prehypertension, in which the individual does not yet have dangerously high blood pressure, but is at significant risk of developing hypertension if steps are not taken to lower the blood pressure. Hypertension can significantly impact virtually every part of the body as the increased force of the blood against the artery walls can severely damage the body's organs, including the heart, brain, eyes, and kidneys, if it goes untreated. Usually there are no apparent symptoms associated with hypertension, but individuals with extremely high blood pressure might experience headaches, vomiting, and difficulty seeing clearly.

Hypertension can usually be treated through the use of a low-salt and low-fat diet along with exercise to bring the individual's blood pressure back down to a reasonable level. People who are being treated for hypertension are usually also advised to stop smoking and drinking to excess, unless it is believed that ceasing these activities will actually put too much additional stress on the individual's body. Persons with significantly higher blood pressures are also often prescribed medication that will help reduce their blood pressure further. There is no way to completely eliminate the risk of hypertension and some factors, including age, race, and family history, can make the individual more predisposed to developing hypertension. However, there are certain factors that individuals can eliminate from their daily activities to significantly lower their risk of developing hypertension. These activities include excessive drinking, smoking, regularly consuming high-salt foods, regular involvement in high-stress activities, and other similar factors that put additional stress on the body.

Dietary Guidelines for Americans

The **Dietary Guidelines for Americans** is a combined publication of the United States Department of Health and Human Services and the United States Department of Agriculture that offers advice to consumers about dietary choices that promote good health and reduce the risk of certain diseases, including hypertension, anemia, and osteoporosis. The Dietary Guidelines for Americans offers advice to consumers on a variety of topics such as weight management, appropriate exercise, food safety, and examples of good sources of certain nutrients. This publication is important because it offers a detailed outline of the kinds of foods that an individual should have in their diets, so they do not need to use additional supplements and vitamins. It also informs consumers of the types of exercise that are necessary for an individual to stay healthy as well as the appropriate manner in which to handle and prepare certain foods to minimize the risk of foodborne illness.

Importance of Vitamins

Vitamin C, also known as ascorbic acid, is important because it helps protect the health of the skin, bones, teeth, cartilage, and blood vessels. Vitamin C protects these areas of the body primarily by acting as an antioxidant that helps reduce the negative effects that oxygen reactions within the body can have on the cells. Vitamin C is also necessary in the production of collagen, which is a protein necessary for skin and cartilage health. Significant vitamin C deficiencies can result in a number of serious health problems including a disorder known as scurvy, in which the body lacks the collagen it requires to maintain the health of the skin. Scurvy ultimately leads to the formation of liver spots on the skin and gums, and can also cause bleeding from all the body's mucous membranes including the nose, lips, ears, and other areas. Common sources of vitamin C include strawberries, oranges, lemons, limes, mangos, grapes, broccoli, potatoes, spinach, liver, and milk.

Vitamin E, and its form tocopherol, is important primarily because it aids in maintaining proper brain function and eye health. It has also been suggested that vitamin E may help reduce the risk of cancer, cataracts, heart disease, and other health conditions as well as helping treat patients that have Parkinson's or Alzheimer's Disease. A significant vitamin E deficiency can result in muscle weakness, blindness, and neurological problems as a result of the body transmitting nerve impulses incorrectly. Common sources of vitamin E include peanuts, hazelnuts, coconuts, corn, asparagus, carrots, tomatoes, fish, peanut butter, and vegetable oils. There are also many multivitamins and supplements that supply vitamin E, but some studies have shown that some synthetic vitamins and supplements may actually be significantly less beneficial or even have a negative impact on the individual when taken in large doses. However, both men and women do require vitamin E, in similar amounts, to continue functioning normally.

B12, and its synthetic form cyanocobalamin, is important because it is necessary for the production of blood cells and aids in maintaining the health of the nervous system. A severe lack of B12 within the body can lead to a variety of conditions including megaloblastic anemia, a condition in which the red blood cells have less hemoglobin and therefore have more difficulty functioning properly. A significant lack of B12 can also lead to severe problems with the nervous system because the lack of B12 causes the disintegration and death of nerve cells. Individuals who lack significant quantities of B12 may develop symptoms such as numbness, tingling, and difficulty with muscle control. Some common sources of B12 include chicken, beef, pork, liver, fish, shellfish, certain breakfast cereals, milk, cheese, eggs, and yogurt. Vegetarians may have difficulty getting enough B12 since the primary sources of B12 are meat products, but B12 supplements and multivitamins can be a good option as well.

Vitamin A, and its derivative retinol, is important because it aids in bone growth, skin health, and the ability to reproduce. Vitamin A also promotes eye health and aids in the production of tears, which prevents the eyes from drying out and washes away bacteria that might cause infections. A vitamin A deficiency can cause the eyes to deteriorate and may lead to conditions such as night blindness, also known as nyctalopia, in which an individual has difficulty seeing in low light environments. Common sources of vitamin A include carrots, sweet potatoes, pumpkins, spinach, beef, pork, chicken, eggs, and broccoli. Both men and women require similar amounts of vitamin A for their bodies to function normally, but men usually require slightly more than women do.

Importance of Fiber

Fiber is an important part of an individual's diet because it helps with bowel movements, digestion, and immune responses. Fiber has also been shown to lower blood cholesterol, help prevent obesity, lower the risk of certain types of cancer including colon cancer, and lower the risk of type 2 diabetes. A significant lack of fiber in an individual's diet can lead to symptoms such as constipation and slower digestion and can cause an individual to have a higher risk of developing certain diseases. Some common sources of fiber include certain breakfast cereals, oatmeal, whole-wheat bread, beans, apples, pears, strawberries, bananas, potatoes, onions, and green beans. Both men and women require similar amounts of fiber to continue functioning properly.

Importance of Protein

Protein is important to the functioning of a healthy individual because it is necessary for the body to produce the amino acids it needs to continue functioning. Most of the amino acids that the body needs are already present in the body, but certain amino acids, known as essential amino acids, can only be produced when the body digests protein. A severe lack of protein is usually caused by malnutrition and can lead to reduced brain function, intellectual disabilities, and an overall weakening of the immune system due to a decrease in the number of white blood cells. It has also been suggested that a significant lack of protein may lead to conditions such as kwashiorkor, which causes significant weight loss, thinning and discolored hair, swelling of the organs, and weakens the responses of the immune system. Some common sources of protein include chicken, beef, wheat, rice, milk, cheese, eggs, peas, beans, peanuts, and peanut butter.

Importance of Iron

Iron is important because it aids in the proper functioning of virtually all the muscles and organs. Iron also allows the body to form hemoglobin, which is a protein in red blood cells that carries oxygen throughout the body. If an individual does not have enough iron in their diet, anemia can result, a condition in which the body is unable to produce hemoglobin. The body may also be unable to produce additional red blood cells if there is a lack of iron, and the individual will be more likely to become fatigued and develop other symptoms and conditions. Common sources of iron include oatmeal, spaghetti, whole wheat bread, sunflower seeds, broccoli, green beans, beets, peas, potatoes, green leafy vegetables, beef, pork, and chicken. Women usually require more iron than men do partially because of the regular blood loss associated with menstruation.

Importance of Calcium

Calcium is important to the development and maintenance of bones and teeth, since a lack of calcium can result in osteoporosis and other bone problems. Calcium is also important to the production of lymph, which is a fluid similar to interstitial fluid that aids in the overall operation of the body, specifically the immune system. Common sources of calcium are milk, cheese, eggs, orange juice, oranges, broccoli, rutabagas, almonds, and other nuts. Calcium can also be obtained through supplements and multivitamins, which can be a good source for people who are allergic to dairy products or have a significant calcium deficiency. Both men and women require similar amounts of calcium, but the amount of calcium required increases as an individual ages.

RDA and RDI

RDA stands for recommended dietary allowance, which is the amount of each vitamin, mineral, or other nutrient that health professionals believe an individual needs to receive daily in order to stay healthy. The RDA has been replaced by the now more commonly used **RDI** or reference daily intake. The RDI is similar to the RDA, but does not recommend different nutrient intakes based on gender and age as the RDA does. The RDI is used to determine the RDV, or recommended daily value, which is printed on virtually every food product in the United States and Canada to inform consumers of the nutritional value, or the lack thereof, that each product offers. These recommended daily values are usually based on a 2000-calorie diet, and since the RDI recommends the same nutrient intake for everyone, there is no difference shown between the intakes necessary for individuals of different age groups or genders. Both the RDA and RDI are important because they allow consumers to determine which foods are best for their diet.

Low Activity and High Activity Individuals

A **low activity** individual is usually considered to be anyone who does not exercise regularly and gets less than 30 minutes of exercise on any given day. A **high activity** individual is usually considered to be anyone who exercises regularly and gets at least 30 to 60 minutes of exercise 4 to 5 times a week. An individual can also be considered high activity if they are in a profession that is physically intense such as warehouse workers, moving company workers, gym teachers, etc. Individuals who exercise more than 30 minutes at a time, but do so only once or twice a week are usually considered mid-level activity persons rather than high or low activity individuals.

Nutritional needs change in a variety of ways as an individual ages, but the major changes involve which vitamins and the number of calories the body requires to keep functioning. Young children usually require around 1000 to 1500 calories a day, but the amount of calories a child requires increases as the child grows. Young teens usually require somewhere between 1600 and 2200 calories a day, depending on their gender and other factors. Individuals entering young adulthood usually require between 2000 and 2400 calories a day. However, after a person reaches age 30, the calorie requirement begins to decrease and continues to do so as they get older. People also require progressively more Vitamins A, C, and E as well as iron and fiber as they age. Individuals over age 50 also require significantly more calcium.

An individual that is more active requires more calories than a person who is less active. A young active child usually requires about the same number of calories as a less active child, but the difference between the calorie needs increases substantially as the children grow. Active young teens require 1600 to 2600 calories, depending on gender and other factors, and active individuals entering young adulthood usually require between 2000 and 3200 calories. As these age ranges show, the calorie needs of an active individual is usually between 400–800 calories higher than a less active person. Active people also require more protein than less active individuals, but usually require similar amounts of Vitamins A, C, and E as well as iron and fiber.

Factors Affecting Nutritional Needs

Some of the major factors that can affect an individual's nutritional needs include:

- **Age of the individual**: The age of an individual plays a major role in the nutritional needs that person has in several ways. As a child grows, for instance, the number of calories the child needs also increases, but after the individual passes a certain age, the number of calories they need decreases. A person's need for specific vitamins and minerals also increases as they get older.
- **Individual's gender**: Gender can affect an individual's nutritional needs; men typically require more protein and more calories than women do, while women usually require significantly more iron than men.
- **Individual's level of activity**: Level of activity also plays a large role in their nutritional needs because an individual who is more active will require a larger number of calories than an individual who less active.

Cholesterol

Cholesterol is a lipid, a type of fat that the body uses to produce both new cells and bile, a substance secreted by the liver that helps the body digest fat. Although the body requires a certain amount of cholesterol to continue functioning normally, excessive amounts of cholesterol can lead to heart and circulatory problems, including a condition known as atherosclerosis, a dangerous condition in which arteries are clogged by deposits of cholesterol. Clogged arteries can cause a variety of other serious problems, such as heart attacks and strokes, because the heart, brain, and many other vital organs cannot receive enough blood to function properly. One of the best ways to avoid too much cholesterol is to stay away from foods that contain high concentrations of saturated fats. Some examples of foods that are high in cholesterol and saturated fats are beef, pork, eggs, milk, butter, cheese, and most snack foods. Some examples of foods that are low in cholesterol and saturated fats include oatmeal, fish, rice, and most fruits and vegetables.

Carbohydrates

Carbohydrates, also known as saccharides, are a group of simple and complex sugars and starches that form an important class of foods in an individual's nutritional needs by supplying energy for the body. Such carbohydrates as the sugar glucose are transported throughout the body via the bloodstream and broken down into energy that keeps the body functioning. Carbohydrates are also important in the function and regulation of the body's immune system and reproductive system. In addition, because carbohydrates aid a person's blood in clotting effectively, they play an essential role in the body's ability to heal. Although many of the body's functions that carbohydrates play a role in can be carried out by proteins and fats as well, carbohydrates are easier for the body to digest and contain less cholesterol than proteins and saturated fats. Examples of foods that are high in carbohydrates include bread, beans, cereals, pasta, potatoes, and rice.

Review Video: Carbohydrates
Visit mometrix.com/academy and enter code: 601714

FATS

Fats are important to the healthy functioning of the body because they allow certain vitamins, including vitamins A, D, E, and K, to be digested and absorbed by the body. These fat-soluble vitamins can be broken down and used by the body only when enough fat is present. In addition, a lack of certain fats in an individual can lead to other vitamin deficiencies. Fats also help maintain the body's temperature; help promote hair, skin, and overall cell health; protect the body's organs; help protect against some diseases; and act as a means of storing energy for the body to use later. However, an excessive amount of fat in the body can adversely affect an individual's health, as an abundance of saturated fats and trans fats can greatly increase the cholesterol level in the blood, which in turn increases an individual's risk of certain heart conditions and other health problems. Some foods that individuals may want to avoid eating in excess because they are high in fat include butter, cream, cheese, lard, milk, and snack foods.

IODINE

Relatively small amounts of **iodine** are important to an individual's health because the element iodine is necessary for the production of thyroid hormones, which the body needs to function normally. A lack of iodine in an individual's diet or an excessive amount of iodine in the body can lead to a variety of symptoms and conditions including depression, fatigue, mental slowness or intellectual disability, excessive weight gain, and goiter, which is an enlargement of the thyroid gland characterized by an extremely swollen neck. Iodine deficiencies are fairly uncommon in the United States and other developed countries because most of the salt used in cooking has been treated with iodine to make sure that individuals ingest enough iodine on a daily basis. Other foods that have high concentrations of iodine include fish, kelp, and most dairy products.

FOOD

Food is essential for the health of an individual, because it satisfies an individual's nutritional needs. Additionally, food provides many people some degree of psychological satisfaction as well. Food is a basic necessity for the successful functioning of an individual; therefore, the body makes a person aware of its need for food by creating a feeling of hunger. When the individual satisfies this hunger by consuming various foods, the body releases hormones that result in the person's feeling a sensation of being full, an indication that the body's need for sustenance has been assuaged. Certain types of foods satisfy an individual's hunger more effectively than other foods. Foods that are high in fiber, protein, and water usually will make an individual feel more satiated, or full. If an individual's body lacks a specific type of nutrient, the body will cause that person to experience a craving for foods that will satisfy that particular nutritional need.

THE NEW PYRAMID

The New Pyramid is the current federal healthy eating guide, formerly MyPlate and the Food Pyramid. It was introduced for the 2025-2030 Dietary Guidelines for Americans. While MyPlate mainly focused on showing how a meal could be divided into different food groups, The New

Pyramid looks more closely at the kinds of foods people choose. It encourages everyone to eat real, whole, nutrient-dense foods as often as possible. This includes such foods as protein, dairy, vegetables, fruits, healthy fats, and whole grains, especially when they are in their natural or minimally processed forms. The guidelines also remind people to limit foods and drinks that are heavily processed or high in added sugars, refined carbohydrates, excess sodium, unhealthy fats, and artificial ingredients. Overall, The New Pyramid is not just about how much of each food group is on the plate. It mainly focuses on the quality of the food chosen and encourages people to build meals around choices that provide important nutrients and support better health throughout their lives.

History of American Dietary Guidelines

Early in 1977, the US Senate Select Committee on Nutrition and Human Needs, then chaired by Senator George McGovern, following extensive reviews of science and discussions, recommended dietary goals consisting of recommendations concerning food and nutrients. The first goal recommended Americans only eat as much energy from food (i.e., calories) as they expended. This goal addressed obesity through balanced consumption. Regarding nutrients, the committee recommended eating more complex carbohydrates and fewer simple (i.e., processed or refined) carbohydrates and decreasing total fat, saturated fat, cholesterol, and sodium. Food goals also included eating more vegetables, fruits, and whole grains and replacing more saturated fats with unsaturated fats. Due to controversy and skepticism from industrial and scientific groups, the US Departments of Agriculture and Health and Human Services (formerly Health, Education, and Welfare) jointly issued a nutrition and health brochure in 1980, partly based on the Surgeon General's 1979 report on health promotion and disease prevention and reflecting research findings about relationships between diet and health. However, this too met with debate.

Despite their straightforward, scientific basis, US Dietary Guidelines issued in 1980 encountered arguments from various industrial and scientific quarters. In response, Congress directed the Departments of Agriculture (USDA) and Health and Human Services (HHS, formerly HEW) to form an advisory committee to solicit formal and informal outside and private-sector advice for subsequent editions. Though the 1985 edition of the Guidelines did not incorporate extensive changes, adding non-federal scientists' input resulted in far less controversy and wider adoption. HHS and USDA formed a second scientific advisory committee in 1989 to review and revise the Guidelines. The 1990 edition reinforced earlier editions' principles, but additionally suggested numerical targets for saturated and total fat amounts, emphasizing these did not apply to a single food or meal, but to eating choices over multiple days. While these first three editions were voluntarily issued, the 1990 National Nutrition Monitoring and related Research Act first legally mandated the Dietary Guidelines report, required a new report every five years, and established a Dietary Guidelines Advisory Committee for that purpose. The 2005 committee adopted systematic methods to review scientific evidence and literature. The 2010 committee extended these, also establishing the Nutrition Evidence Library to support its work with a comprehensive, evidence-based review process.

Nutrients, Carbohydrates, Fats, Protein, Vitamins, and Minerals Found in Foods

Carbohydrates are starches, fibers, and sugars in foods from which the body manufactures glucose, the blood sugar used to fuel all activities of the body, including the brain. Glucose is accessed immediately, or stored in the muscles and liver for future use. Fats are necessary to normal bodily functions, but only 20-35 percent of the human diet need be from fats (preferably oils, not solid fats; and unsaturated, not saturated or trans fats). USDA recommends eating below 10 percent of calories in saturated fats, and avoiding trans fats. (Trans fats are found in partially hydrogenated oils.) Humans need to eat foods with protein, which our bodies digest into amino acids to rebuild all organs, tissues, and cells, which contain protein that is continually broken down and replaced. Animal proteins are complete protein sources with all essential amino acids. Vegetable proteins are incomplete sources, but combining complementary vegetable proteins can yield complete protein. Ten to 35 percent of daily calories should be protein; Americans typically eat enough. Vitamins and minerals are important to health; for instance, vitamin D aids calcium absorption, and calcium promotes strong bone formation. Supplements are available, but eating a nutritious and varied diet usually provides enough vitamins and minerals.

FAT

Fats are divided into two main categories: saturated and unsaturated. Saturated fats are mostly found in meat, lard, butter, coconut, and palm oil. Doctors consider these fats to be the most hazardous to health because they increase the risk of heart disease and certain kinds of cancer. Unsaturated fats include sunflower oil, corn oil, olive oil, and canola oil. The last two oils are called monounsaturated fats and are particularly good for the body because they lower cholesterol. Recent research has concluded that the most harmful kinds of fats are trans fats, which are formed when liquid vegetable oil is processed to make table spreads and cooking fats. Trans fats have been consistently shown to create buildup in arteries, a process which can impair heart health.

Many fats can increase cholesterol, a substance in the body which has consistently been linked with heart disease. Cholesterol has many positive uses in the body, like helping the liver operate and helping to form many hormones, but if cholesterol becomes too abundant, it can build up in the arteries and impede the flow of blood. Research has shown that saturated fats cause a more significant buildup of cholesterol than unsaturated fats or other foods that contain cholesterol. In order to minimize cholesterol in the diet, individuals should cut back on fats altogether, but especially limit their intake of saturated fats. Monounsaturated fats, like canola and olive oil, are a good, low-cholesterol source of fat.

FIBER

Whole grains, fruits, and vegetables are all excellent sources of fiber. Fiber can be either insoluble or soluble. Insoluble fibers (cellulose and lignin, for example) speed digestion and can reduce the risk of colon cancer and heart disease. Wheat and corn bran, leafy vegetables, and fruit and vegetable skins are all great sources of insoluble fiber. Soluble fibers (pectins and gums, for example) lower cholesterol levels and help manage the level of blood sugar. They can be found in the pulp of fruits and in vegetables, oats, beans, and barley. Doctors warn that most Americans do not eat nearly enough fiber. However, increasing fiber in your diet should be done gradually, as a sudden increase in fiber can result in bloating, cramps, and diarrhea.

WATER

A person should drink 7 to 10 average sized glasses of water daily. Water is probably the most important substance a person can consume. Water carries nutrients throughout the body and regulates body temperature. Water lubricates joints, aids digestion, and helps speed waste matter out of the body. Losing even 5% of the body's water causes immediate physical symptoms, like dizziness, fatigue, and headache; losing 15% of the body's water can be fatal. The normal daily loss is between 64 and 80 ounces of water a day, which is equal to about 9 large glasses of water. Many fruits and vegetables contain helpful water, but people should still consume the recommended amount of water each day. People who are active, live at a high altitude, or travel a great deal should be sure to drink even more water.

Water Supply

Even though Americans have generally been able to rely on the water supply, in recent years some concerns have been raised about the prevalence of potentially dangerous chemicals in water. Fluoride, which has greatly improved dental health by strengthening teeth since it was added to the water supply, may be damaging to bone strength if it is consumed in great volume. Chlorine, which is often added to water to kill bacteria, may increase the risk of bladder cancer. One of the most dangerous chemicals that can affect water is lead, which is known to leach from pipes and enter the drinking supply. High amounts of lead in the body can cause serious damage to the brain and heart.

Review Video: Dehydration
Visit mometrix.com/academy and enter code: 283651

Alcoholism

The National Council on Alcoholism and Drug Dependence considers alcoholism as a disease that is influenced by social, environmental, and genetic factors. The common features of alcoholism are the inability to control consumption, continued drinking despite negative consequences, and distorted thinking patterns (like irrational denial). It is important to note that alcoholism is not simply the result of a weak will but is a physiological state that requires medical treatment so that it can be controlled. Many individuals may have a problem with alcoholism but not realize it if they are still functioning well overall and only drink in social situations. Alcoholics tend to be those who, even when they aren't drinking, place an undue amount of psychological emphasis on alcohol.

Drug Abuse

A drug is any chemical substance that changes the way a person acts or feels. Drugs may affect a person's mental, physical, or emotional state. Though many drugs are taken to improve the condition of the body or to remedy personal problems, drugs can also undermine health by distorting a person's mind and weakening a person's body. According to the World Health Organization, drug abuse is any excessive drug use that is not approved by the medical profession. The use of some drugs in any quantity is considered abuse; other drugs must be taken in large quantities before they are considered to have been abused. There are health risks involved with the use of any drug, legal or illegal, insofar as they introduce a foreign substance into the balanced system of physical health.

Appetite

The feeling of hunger can be caused by up to 12 different hormones and areas of the brain. There is even some speculation that the size of an individual's fat cells may cause them to feel hungry. The appetite is the physiological desire to eat, and though it is thought to be the body's means of avoiding failure, it can also be stimulated when the body does not really need food. Humans tend to stop eating when they reach the point of satiety, in which they are no longer hungry and feel full. Scientists have advanced the set-point theory of appetite, which contends that each individual has an internal system that is geared to regulate hunger and satiety so as to keep body fat at a certain rate.

Health and Wellness

Health

Quite simply, **health** is the state of being sound in mind, body, and spirit. According to the World Health Organization, health is not only the absence of disease, but the presence of physical, mental, and social well-being. When assessing an individual's health, a professional is likely to examine them from a physical, psychological, spiritual, social, intellectual, or environmental standpoint. Although every individual has their own standard of health, it is common for people to recognize the following characteristics as healthy: an optimistic outlook in life, the ability to relax, a supportive home life, a clean environment, a satisfying job, freedom from pain and illness, and the energy necessary to enjoy life.

Wellness

Health professionals refer to the highest state of health as **wellness**. Wellness has a number of definitions: it may mean enjoying life, or having a defined purpose in life and being able to work towards it, or it may mean deliberately taking the steps necessary to avoid disease and maximize health. Wellness is different from health in that it means actively enhancing health, not just maintaining good health. Total wellness depends on psychological, physical, and social factors. In the general model for wellness, all of these factors combine to produce the individual's complete level of wellness. Indeed, part of the reason why health professionals promote the idea of wellness is to show people that all the areas of their lives depend on one another.

Psychological Health

In order to achieve **psychological health**, you must have an accurate and favorable impression of yourself. Having healthy self-esteem does not mean overestimating your talents and value; it means feeling good about your role in life and expecting that you will have the personal resources to deal with any adversity. A person who has a reasonable concept of themselves will be able to tolerate the faults of others, based upon the knowledge gained from self-reflection. Part of establishing a realistic but positive view of the world is accepting that there are many things that you will be unable to change in life, and that rather than making yourself miserable about them, you can direct your attention to those things that are under your control.

Physical Education

The meaning of the phrase "**physical education**" may seem obvious at first glance, but it is quite possible for individuals to have very distinct ideas of what physical education entails. Physical education, by most accounts, is composed of exercise (the use of the body), play (the action generated by the exertion of the body), games (competitions of any kind), leisure (freedom from the responsibilities of work), recreation (any activity that refreshes the mind and body after work), sport (physical activities performed for pleasure or achievement), and athletics (organized, competitive activities). So, a general definition of physical education might be that it is the process whereby an individual improves their physical, mental, and social skill through physical activity.

Personal Fitness

Personal fitness is particular to the individual. Some people may be considered fit when they can run for a mile without stopping, while others may be athletic enough to accomplish that feat without really being in shape. Most people will acquire a sense of their own fitness only after spending a great deal of time exercising, setting fitness goals, and working to achieve them. However, those who want more objective data on their physical condition may submit to testing at a sports medicine laboratory. There, they will have their muscular and cardiovascular endurance measured on a treadmill, their body fat measured in a submersion tank, and their flexibility tested through a variety of trials.

Cardiovascular Fitness

An individual's **cardiovascular fitness** is the ability of their heart to pump blood through the body at the necessary rate. Proper cardiovascular fitness can be achieved through aerobic exercise: that is, any activity during which the amount of oxygen taken into the body is equal to or more than the amount the body is using. Jogging, walking, or riding a bike are all examples of aerobic activity. The heart also gets an excellent workout during anaerobic exercise, in which the body takes in less oxygen than it needs to maintain the activity. Sprinting or swimming fast can be anaerobic exercises, if they leave the person breathless. Nonaerobic exercise, like bowling or golf, does not challenge the heart and lungs and therefore will not improve cardiovascular fitness.

Muscle Strength and Endurance

Developing healthy muscles is not simply a matter of lifting the heaviest possible object. The ability to use your muscles over and over without getting tired is also an important part of physical fitness. Developing **muscular strength** and **endurance** will help make body tissue firmer and more resilient. Well-maintained muscles tend to work more efficiently, and they can withstand more strain. Furthermore, muscular development aids in circulation, with the result that the whole body absorbs and makes use of nutrients in the blood more quickly. Strength and endurance training has also been shown to be one of the most effective ways to lose weight, as developed muscles burn more calories than fat does.

Exercising Muscles

Muscles are in a constant state of change. If muscles are not used, they will atrophy and weaken; on the other hand, if they are regularly exercised, they will grow stronger and possibly larger. Muscles are best exercised when they are overloaded or asked to do more than they usually do. When you are training your muscles, you will need to gradually increase the amount of the weight or the number of repetitions to ensure that your muscles are always receiving a challenge. Many fitness professionals contend that a good muscular workout will be somewhat painful because muscles can only be developed by exceeding their normal requirements. However, not every kind of pain is profitable for a muscular workout, and individuals should be careful to distinguish muscular fatigue from injury, particularly when they are lifting heavy loads.

Recreation Safety Laws

A number of laws exist to ensure the safety of individuals when they engage in recreational activities. For instance, an individual may not be intoxicated while driving a boat. There are also laws governing the use of jet-skis, wave runners, snowmobiles, and all-terrain vehicles. The federal government cites these last vehicles as particularly dangerous for young, untrained, or intoxicated drivers. A set of regulations governs the use of the national and state parks (e.g., restrictions on the building of fires). The federal government recently reported a sharp increase in the number of in-line skating and skateboarding injuries; skaters are now denied access to many recreational areas because of the increased safety risk.

Vital Signs

Every individual should be able to identify the **vital signs** and know how to measure them. The four common measures considered to be vital signs are body temperature, blood pressure, pulse rate, and respiration rate. Body temperature can be taken with a thermometer and should register between 96º and 99.9º Fahrenheit, depending on the time of day and sex (women tend to have slightly higher temperatures). Measuring blood pressure requires some equipment; a normal blood pressure is between 120/70 and 140/90, depending on age and sex. A normal pulse rate is ranges between 60 and 80 beats per minute. For athletes, resting pulse rates can be even lower. A normal respiration rate is between 15 to 20 breaths a minute.

Warming Up and Cooling Down

There are important reasons for warming up before and cooling down after exercise. For one thing, performance is always enhanced by warming up. Muscles tend to work more effectively when their temperature has been slightly raised; they are also more resistant to strains and tears at a higher temperature. Warming up directs the blood to working muscles and gives the heart time to adjust to the increased demands of the muscles. Warming up also stimulates the secretion of synovial fluid into the joints, which makes them less likely to suffer wear and tear. Warming up should include slow stretching and low-impact cardiovascular exercise. Cooling down is important for easing the body's transition to a normal resting condition. By stretching and slowly decreasing cardiovascular workload, the heart is aided in its readjustment.

Recreation Versus Competition

One of the perennial issues facing physical educators is whether activities should be promoted as forms of recreation or as competition. If competition is to be the dominant feature, then activities must have explicit rules, a formal way of keeping score, and identifiable winners and losers. When students are taught activities for competition, the emphasis will be on practicing specific skills and avoiding mistakes as much as possible. When sports are taught as recreation, participation is the most important factor for students. Each student should get an equal amount of experience and performance time, regardless of their skill level. Although score is typically not kept in strictly recreational activities, students may receive certificates for good sportsmanship or diligent participation.

Health Education as a Community Service

In a general sense, all of health education can be seen as community service. By teaching positive health behaviors and promoting good health to students, health teachers are improving the quality of life for everyone in the community. More specifically, though, the Center for Disease Control has recommended that health educators use their special training to improve health through work outside of school. Many health educators participate in fundraising for health charities, give speeches on health-related topics, or work in the community to generate enthusiasm for exercise and nutrition. According to the Code of Ethics for health educators, it is imperative for those with knowledge and skills to advance positive health behaviors whenever possible and, thus, help their community.

Aerobic Fitness

A minimum of **aerobic fitness** has been achieved when you are able to exercise three times a week at 65% of your maximum heart rate. The easiest means of achieving this level of fitness is by running for 30 minutes three or four times a week. Moderate aerobic fitness is achieved by exercising four or more times a week for at least 30 minutes at a heart rate that is 75% or more of maximum. This level of aerobic fitness is appropriate for athletes who are seeking to play vigorous sports like football or tennis. Maximum aerobic fitness can only be achieved by working close to maximum heart rate several times a week and by exercising vigorously almost every day. In order to achieve this level of fitness, you must consistently work beyond your anaerobic threshold. A good way to do this is having interval training or brief, high-intensity workouts.

Skeletal System

The **skeletal system** is composed of about 200 bones which, along with the attached ligaments and tendons, create a protective and supportive network for the body's muscles and soft tissues. There are two main components of the skeletal system: the axial skeleton and the appendicular skeleton. The axial skeleton includes the skull, spine, ribs, and sternum; the appendicular skeleton includes the pelvis, shoulders, and the various arm and leg bones attached to these. The skeleton does not move, but it is pulled in various directions by the muscles. There are few differences between the male and female skeleton: the bones of a male tend to be a bit larger and heavier than those of the female, who will have a wider pelvic cavity.

Review Video: Skeletal System
Visit mometrix.com/academy and enter code: 256447

Lymphatic System

The **lymphatic system** is connected to the cardiovascular system through a network of capillaries. The lymphatic system filters out organisms that cause disease, controls the production of disease-fighting antibodies, and produces white blood cells. The lymphatic system also prevents body tissues from swelling by draining fluids from them. Two of the most important areas in this system are the right lymphatic duct and the thoracic duct. The right lymphatic duct moves the immunity-bolstering lymph fluid through the top half of the body, while the thoracic duct moves lymph throughout the lower half. The spleen, thymus, and lymph nodes all generate and store the chemicals which form lymph and which are essential to protecting the body from disease.

Nervous System

The **nervous system** collects information for the body and indicates what the body should do to survive in the present conditions. For instance, it is the nervous system that administers a bad feeling when the body is cold, and then sends a more positive message when a person warms up. These important messages are sent by the nerves, which vary in size and cover the entire body. The central nervous system is composed of the brain and spinal cord, and the peripheral nervous system is composed of the rest of the body, including those organs which a person does not voluntarily control. The peripheral nervous system is divided into sympathetic and parasympathetic systems, which counterbalance one another to allow for smooth function.

Review Video: Function of the Nervous System
Visit mometrix.com/academy and enter code: 708428

Digestive System

The **digestive system** is composed of organs that convert food into energy. This process begins with the teeth, which grind food into small particles that are easy to digest. Food is then carried through the pharynx (throat) and esophagus to the stomach. In the stomach, it is partially digested by strong acids and enzymes. From there, food passes through the small and large intestines, the rectum, and out through the anus. On this journey, it will be mixed with numerous chemicals so that it can be absorbed into the blood and lymph system. Some food will be converted into immediate energy, and some will be stored for future use; whatever cannot be used by the body will be expelled as waste.

Review Video: Gastrointestinal System
Visit mometrix.com/academy and enter code: 378740

Muscular System

The muscles of the body are attached to the skeleton by tendons and other connective tissues. Muscles exert force and move the bones of the body by converting chemical energy into contractions. Every muscular act is the result of some muscle growing shorter. The muscles themselves are composed of millions of tiny proteins. Muscles are stimulated by nerves that link them to the brain and spinal cord. There are three types of muscles: cardiac muscles are found only in the heart and pump the blood through the body; smooth muscles surround or are part of internal organs; skeletal muscles are those a person controls voluntarily. Skeletal muscles are the most common tissue in the body, accounting for between 25 and 40% of body weight.

Review Video: Muscular System
Visit mometrix.com/academy and enter code: 967216

Endocrine System

The **endocrine system** creates and secretes the hormones that accomplish a wide variety of tasks in the body. The endocrine system is made up of glands. These glands produce chemicals that regulate metabolism, growth, and sexual development. Glands release hormones directly into the bloodstream, where they are then directed to the various organs and tissues of the body. The endocrine system is generally considered to include the pituitary, thyroid, parathyroid, and adrenal glands, as well as the pancreas, ovaries, and testes. The endocrine system regulates its level of hormone production by monitoring the activity of hormones; when it senses that a certain hormone is active, it reduces or stops production of that hormone.

Review Video: Endocrine System
Visit mometrix.com/academy and enter code: 678939

Circulatory System

The **circulatory system** is composed of the heart, the blood vessels, and the blood. This system circulates the blood throughout the body, giving nutrients and other essential materials to the body cells and removing waste products. Arteries carry blood away from the heart, and veins carry blood back to the heart. Within body tissues, tiny capillaries distribute blood to the various body cells. The heart takes oxygenated blood from the lungs and distributes it to the body; when blood comes back bearing carbon dioxide, the heart sends it to the lungs to be expelled. Other organs not always considered to be a part of this system (for instance, the kidneys and spleen) help to remove some impurities from the blood.

Review Video: Cardiovascular System
Visit mometrix.com/academy and enter code: 376581

Hormone System

Hormones are the chemicals that motivate the body to do certain things. They are produced in the organs that make up the endocrine system. With the exception of the sex organs, males and females have identical endocrine systems. The actions of the hormones are determined by the hypothalamus, an area of the brain about the size of a pea. The hypothalamus sends messages to the pituitary gland, which is directly beneath it. The pituitary gland turns on and off the various glands that produce hormones. Hormones, once released, are carried to their targets by the bloodstream, at which point they motivate cells and organs to action. Hormones can influence the way a person looks, feels, behaves, or matures.

Cartilage

The areas of bones that are close to joints are covered in a shiny connective tissue known as **cartilage**. Cartilage supports the joint structure and protects the fragile bone tissue underneath. Cartilage is susceptible to injury because it is subject to gravitational pressure as well as pressure born of joint movement itself. Long-term stress to cartilage can result in rheumatoid arthritis and osteoarthritis. There are no blood vessels in cartilage; nutrients are delivered by the synovial fluid, and from nearby blood vessels. Cartilage contains a huge number of spongy fibers because it needs to absorb a great deal of shock. Especially resilient cartilage, known as fibrocartilage, is found between the vertebrae and in the knees, among other places.

Ligaments

Ligaments are dense bundles of fibers running parallel to one another from one bone in a joint to another. Ligaments are a part of the joint capsule, although they may also connect to other nearby bones that are not part of the joint. Ligaments are not like muscles; they cannot contract. Instead, ligaments passively strengthen and support the joints by absorbing some of the tension of movement. Ligaments do contain nerve cells which are sensitive to position and speed of movement, and so ligaments can hurt. One function of this pain is to alert the person to an unnatural or dangerous movement of the joint. Ligaments may also be strained or rupture if they are placed under unnecessary or violent stress.

Muscle Tissue

Muscle tissue is made up of bundles of fibers which are held in position and separated by various partitions. These partitions range from large (deep fascia, epimysium) to small (perimysium, endomysium), and often extend beyond the length of the muscle and form tendons connecting to a bone. Each muscle cell is extremely long and has a large amount of nuclei. Every muscle cell contains a number of smaller units called sarcomeres; these contain thick filaments of the protein myosin and thin filaments of the protein actin. Muscle tissue contracts when a nerve stimulates the muscle and the thin filaments compress within the sarcomere, causing a general muscle contraction.

Setting Goals

Individuals who are most likely to make positive permanent changes in their health set realistic goals along the way. When setting goals, individuals should identify what resources (time, money, and effort) are available to achieve them. Individuals should also identify the potential barriers to success and consider ways to minimize or remove these problems. It is always better to set a number of small, attainable goals rather than goals that may be difficult to achieve.

Physical Fitness

Physical fitness is the body's ability to perform all of its tasks and still have some reserve energy in case of an emergency. People who are physically fit can meet all of their daily physical needs, have a realistic and positive image of themselves, and are working to protect themselves against future health problems. Physical fitness has three main components: flexibility, cardiovascular fitness, and muscular strength or endurance. Some other factors, like agility and balance, are also often considered when assessing physical fitness. The benefits of pursuing physical fitness throughout life are not only physical but mental and emotional; regular exercise is proven to reduce the risk of disease and increase life expectancy.

Flexibility

A person's **flexibility** is their range of motion around particular joints. An individual's flexibility will vary according to age, gender, and posture. Some individuals may be less flexible because of bone spurs, and some individuals may be less flexible because they are overweight. Typically, an individual's flexibility will increase through childhood until adolescence, at which point joint mobility slows and diminishes for the rest of the individual's life. Muscles and the connective tissue around them (tendons and ligaments) will contract and become tighter if they are not used to their potential. Lack of flexibility can lead to a buildup of tension in the muscles and can increase the risk of injury during exercise.

Heart, Lungs, and Bones

Maintaining physical fitness has a number of advantages besides improving personal appearance. It has been shown time and again that habitual exercise is the best way to prevent coronary death. In fact, individuals who don't exercise are twice as likely as active individuals to die of a heart attack. Exercise makes the lungs more efficient, as they are able to take in more oxygen and make better use of it. This provides the body with more available energy. Exercise also benefits the bones. Individuals who do not exercise are more likely to have weak or brittle bones, and they are more prone to osteoporosis, in which bones lose their mineral density and become dangerously soft.

Mood, Disease Prevention, and Body Weight

The benefits of regular exercise are both physical and mental. It is well documented that frequent exercise improves a person's mood, increases energy, focus, and alertness, and reduces anxiety. In fact, long workouts cause the release of mood-elevating chemicals called endorphins into the brain. Exercise also reduces the risk of disease. By aiding in the proper digestion, exercise reduces the risk of colon and rectal cancers. Studies have also indicated that women who exercise are less likely to develop breast cancer. Finally, exercise is beneficial because it helps people lose weight and keep it off. The body's metabolism remains elevated for a prolonged period after exercise, which means food is processed more quickly and efficiently. In addition, regular exercise helps suppress the appetite.

Nutrition and Exercise

For most people, the balanced diet depicted in realfood.gov's New Pyramid will supply all the healthy nutrients the body needs to maintain a program of physical fitness. However, individuals who are seriously testing their endurance by exercising for periods of more than an hour at a time will need to increase their intake of complex carbohydrates, which keep the level of blood sugar stable and increase the amount of available glycogen. Contrary to popular thought, heavy workouts do not require a diet high in protein, and in fact, consuming too much protein can put a severe strain on the kidneys and liver. Similarly, most health experts discourage the use of dietary supplements and body-building foods unless under supervision because these products can easily result in nutritional imbalances.

Water and Exercise

Water is the most important thing for a person to consume before, during, and after exercise. On hot days, active people can sweat up to a quart of water. If you become dehydrated, your heart will have a difficult time providing oxygen and nutrients to muscles. Even sports drinks cannot provide the hydrating effect of cool water because the sodium, sugar, and potassium in them delay their absorption into the body. Salt tablets should be avoided as well; they are potentially dangerous and unnecessary. Although people do lose a bit of sodium when they sweat, this is more than offset by the huge amount of salt in the average American diet.

Review Video: Dehydration
Visit mometrix.com/academy and enter code: 283651

First-Aid Tips and Supplies

Since it is necessary to act fast when an emergency happens, it is a good idea to think ahead and have a plan in place. If you are in a public place, you may want to begin by shouting for help to see if a doctor is available. Someone should immediately dial 911. Do not attempt any resuscitation techniques unless you are trained. If you have a car and it is appropriate, you should immediately take the victim to the nearest hospital. Furthermore, every home should have some basic first-aid supplies. A good first-aid kit will include bandages, sterile gauze pads, scissors, adhesive tape, calamine lotion, cotton balls, thermometer, ipecac syrup (to induce vomiting), a sharp needle, and safety pins.

Smog

Smog is the informal name given to the combination of smoke, gases, and fog that accumulates in major industrial or metropolitan areas. Most smog is created by motor vehicles, wood-burning stoves, industrial factories, and electric utilities plants. Gray smog, which is mainly sulfur dioxide, is common in the eastern United States because of the high concentration of industry. This kind of smog acts like cigarette smoke on the lungs, impairing the ability of the cilia to expel particulates. Brown smog comes from automobiles and is mainly composed of nitrogen dioxide. Ozone, one of the other components of brown smog, can impair the immune system. Automobiles are also known to produce carbon monoxide, which diminishes the ability of the red blood cells to carry oxygen.

Pollution

Many people do not consider **pollution** a personal health issue, but polluted air and water can affect every aspect of a person's life. Scientists define pollution as any change in the air, soil, or water that impairs its ability to host life. Most pollution is the byproduct of human acts. Some of the common health problems associated with pollution are nasal discharge, eye irritation, constricted air passages, birth defects, nausea, coughing, and cancer. Environmental agents that change the DNA of living cells are called mutagens, and they can lead to the development of cancer. Pollutants that can pass through the placenta of a woman and cause damage to an unborn child are called teratogens.

Exercise and Weight Loss

Despite the appeal of quick solutions to obesity, exercise remains the best way to reduce weight and maintain weight loss. Many people think that increasing exercise will make them want to eat more; in actuality, frequent exercise tends to reduce the appetite, and since it raises the rate of metabolism, it also helps keep weight off. There are numerous other advantages to exercise in regard to weight; exercise burns off fat reserves and increases muscle mass. Since muscle tends to use calories more quickly than fat, this means it will be more difficult for the individual to put on pounds of fat. In study after study, individuals who exercise regularly are shown to be more likely to lose weight and keep it off.

Communicable and Non-Communicable Diseases

Communicable diseases are those that are caused by microorganisms and can be transferred from one infected person or animal to a previously uninfected person or animal. Although some diseases are passed on by direct contact with an infected individual, many can be spread through close proximity: airborne bacteria or viruses account for most communication of disease. Some examples of communicable disease are measles, smallpox, influenza, and scarlet fever. Some communicable diseases require specific circumstances for transmission; for instance, tetanus requires the presence of infected soil or dirt. Any disease that cannot be transferred from one person or animal to another is considered non-communicable.

Infectious and Non-Infectious Diseases

Infectious diseases are those that are caused by a virus, bacterium, or parasite. Infectious diseases are distinguished from **non-infectious diseases** in that they stem from biological causes, rather than from physical or chemical causes (as in the case of burns or poisoning). An infectious disease will always have an agent (something that has the disease and spreads it to others) and a vector (a way of transmitting the disease). In the case of malaria, for instance, a parasite contains the disease, and it is introduced to the body when a mosquito carrying it places it in the bloodstream. The vector of an infectious disease does not need to be biological; many diseases are transmitted through water, for example.

Viruses

Viruses are the smallest of the pathogens, but they are also the most difficult to destroy. Viruses consist of a small bit of nucleic acid (either DNA or RNA) inside a coating of protein. Viruses are unable to reproduce by themselves, so they infest the reproductive systems of cells already in the body and command them to make new viral cells. These new cells are then sent to other parts of the body. Some of the most common viruses are influenza, herpes, hepatitis, and papilloma. It is difficult to treat viruses without also damaging the cells that they are using. Antibiotics, for instance, have no effect on viruses. Special antiviral drugs must be taken, and even these do not entirely eliminate the presence of the virus.

Bacteria

Bacteria are simple, one-celled organisms and are the most common microorganism and pathogen. Most bacteria do not cause disease; in fact, many bacteria are important to body processes. Bacteria can harm the body when they release enzymes that digest other body cells or when they produce toxins. Since bacteria are quite different from normal body cells, they can usually be effectively treated with antibiotics. However, not just any antibiotic can be used to treat every bacterial infection; a doctor must determine the particular strain of bacteria that is causing the problem before they write a prescription. Over time, bacteria may become resistant to antibiotics, so it is best not to take too much of this effective treatment.

Immune System

The body uses a number of different weapons to try to defeat infections. Most obviously, the skin repels most invaders. Many substances produced by the body (like mucus, saliva, and tears) also fight against infection. When these methods are ineffective, however, the **immune system** goes to work. The immune system consists of parts of the lymphatic system like the spleen, thymus gland, and lymph nodes, and vessels called lymphatics that work to filter impurities out of the body. The spleen is where antibodies are made, as well as the place where old red blood cells are disposed. The thymus gland fortifies white blood cells with the ability to find and destroy invaders. The lymph nodes filter our bacteria and other pathogens.

Whenever an antigen, or infecting substance, enters the body, the immune system immediately goes to work to defeat it. Initially, the T cells fight the antigen while assisted by macrophages (cells that scavenge for foreign or weakened cells). While this battle is raging, the B cells create antibodies to join in. Many pathogens will be transported to the lymph nodes, where a reserve store of antibodies will eliminate them. It is for this reason that the lymph nodes often become swollen during cold and flu season. If the antigens find some success, the body will rush a greater blood supply to the infected area, enriching the supply of oxygen and nutrients. In the event that the pathogens are able to contaminate the blood stream, the infection becomes systemic and much more dangerous.

Review Video: Immune System
Visit mometrix.com/academy and enter code: 622899

Allergies

An **allergy** is a hypersensitivity or overreaction to some substance in a person's environment or diet; it is the most common kind of immune disorder. There are many different symptoms of an allergic reaction, but the most common are sneezing, hives, eye irritation, vomiting, and nasal congestion. In some extreme cases, the person may collapse and even die. Allergic triggers, or allergens, can be anything from peanuts to pollen, or from insect bites to mold. Although there is no way to reverse or eliminate a personal allergy, science has made progress in treating the allergic reaction. These days, it is possible to be treated for an allergic reaction without becoming drowsy or sluggish.

IMMUNIZATIONS

Despite the overwhelming evidence supporting the use of **immunization** in preventing potentially life-threatening diseases, many Americans still neglect to get the basic immunizations. At present, the American Academy of Pediatrics recommends that every child be immunized against measles, mumps, smallpox, rubella, diphtheria, tetanus, and hepatitis B. Some vaccinations will need to be repeated on a certain schedule. Basically, a vaccination is the intentional introduction of a small amount of an antigen into the body. This stimulates the immune system to learn how to fight that particular antigen. There are certain vaccinations that a pregnant woman should not get, and a person should never be vaccinated if they are currently sick.

COMMON COLD

The **common cold** is one of the most pesky and irritating of viruses, though it is rarely a great risk to long-term health. One reason the cold is so difficult to fight is that there are over 200 varieties of the virus, so the body is never able to develop a comprehensive immunity. The cold virus is typically spread through the air or through contact. There is no completely effective medical treatment, either. Indeed, doctors warn that taking aspirin and acetaminophen may actually suppress the antibodies that the body needs to fight the infection and may therefore contribute to some symptoms. There is also no conclusive evidence to support taking vitamin C in large doses. Antihistamines, which many people credit with relieving the symptoms of the common cold, may make the user drowsy.

CANCER

Cancer is the uncontrolled growth and spread of abnormal cells throughout the body. Cancer cells, unlike the regular cells of the body, do not follow the instructions encoded in the body's DNA. Instead, these cells reproduce themselves quickly, creating neoplasms, or tumors. A tumor may be either benign, when it is not considered dangerous, or malignant (cancerous). Unless they are stopped, cancer cells continue to grow, crowding out normal cells in a process called infiltration. Cancer cells can also metastasize, or spread to the other parts of the body by entering the bloodstream or lymphatic system. The gradual overtaking of the body by these cancer cells will eventually make it impossible to sustain human life.

Every cancer has some characteristics in common with other cancers, but it may be more or less treatable depending on its particular nature. The most common forms of cancer are carcinoma, sarcoma, leukemia, and lymphoma. **Carcinoma** is the most common kind of cancer; it originates in the cells that line the internal organs and the outside of the body. **Sarcomas** are those cancers that develop in the connective and supportive tissues of the body, namely bones, muscles, and blood vessels. **Leukemias** are cancers that originate in the blood-creating parts of the body: the spleen, bone marrow, and the lymph nodes. **Lymphomas** are cancers that originate in the cells of the lymph system where impurities are filtered out.

By now, most Americans are aware that the risk of developing cancer is increased more by cigarette smoking than by any other single behavior. Not only do cigarettes lead to lung cancer, but they also lead to cancer of the mouth, pharynx, larynx, esophagus, pancreas, and bladder. The risk of developing cancer is not limited to cigarettes: pipes, smokeless tobacco, and cigars all put a person at risk. Second-hand smoke has a similar effect; scientists have shown that individuals who are exposed to environmental smoke for more than three hours a day are three times more likely to develop cancer than those not exposed. In addition to tobacco, other acknowledged carcinogens are asbestos, dark hair dye, nickel, and vinyl chloride. Individuals should always try to make certain their living and working spaces are well ventilated to reduce the harmful substances in the air.

Hygiene

Besides helping you maintain an attractive appearance, **hygiene** is essential for keeping you healthy and free of disease. The body is usually covered with a certain amount of bacteria, but if this number is allowed to grow too high, you may place yourself at risk for disease. Individuals who fail to regularly wash their hair are more likely to have head lice, and those who fail to properly clean their genitals are more susceptible to urinary tract infections. Good hygiene also reduces an individual's contagiousness when sick. Hygiene is especially important when dealing with food: failing to wash everything involved in the preparation of a meal can result in the spread of bacterial infections like *E. coli* and hepatitis A.

To stay clean and reduce the risk of disease, students should practice daily basic hygiene. Everyone should wash hair and body daily and should wash the hands more frequently than that. Teeth should be brushed between one and three times daily. Always wash hands before eating, avoid spitting or nose-picking, and cover your mouth when sneezing. Try to avoid coming into contact with any bodily fluids, and keep clothes and living space clean. Finally, avoid putting your fingers in your mouth, and try not to touch any animals before eating.

Similarities Between Basic Food Preparation and Medical Hygiene

There are a few basic hygiene habits that every individual should practice when preparing food or performing basic medical procedures. Always clean off the areas where food will be prepared, and wash your hands after touching any uncooked foods. Do not use the same tools to prepare different foods. Always refrigerate foods before and after they are used. Label stored food to indicate when it was produced. Dispose of any uneaten food that cannot be stored. When performing basic medical procedures, always use sterile bandages and any necessary protective clothing, like masks, gloves, or eyewear. Always make sure any medical waste, like used bandages, is disposed of securely.

Meal Planning and Service

Ethics and Religion

An individual's religious, moral, and ethical beliefs can play a large part in their diet because some beliefs can result in the exclusion of certain foods. Ethical and moral considerations such as preventing animal cruelty or showing disapproval of environmentally unfriendly practices that are used to acquire certain types of food can lead some individuals to reduce the amount of certain foods they consume, such as meat, or eliminate those foods from their diet completely. For example, many individuals who choose to be vegetarians or vegans usually do so to avoid supporting what they believe to be the unethical slaughter of animals.

Religious considerations can also determine a person's dietary choices, as some religions dictate what sort of foods the members of that faith can consume. People practicing Judaism, for instance, can consume only kosher foods, which are foods that conform to a series of guidelines established by the faith and include restrictions related to how an animal was slaughtered, what type of animal was slaughtered, and who prepared the food.

Ethnicity

Ethnicity can play an important role in the foods that an individual includes in their diet because people living in different regions of the world usually have different customs regarding the foods that they eat and have different foods commonly available as well. For example, individuals who live in a country like Japan that has easy access to waters suitable for fishing will typically consume significantly more fish than individuals who live in countries that are landlocked. Individuals who have immigrated to another country or who are descendents of immigrants will often include foods in their diet that are traditional foods from their native countries even if those foods are not easily accessible in their new home. People in some regions may include foods in their diets that are not based on how readily available a particular food is, but rather this diet is based on the culture's customary eating habits, as seen in France, where the population as a whole tends to eat foods that are fresh rather than processed.

Planning a Nutritional Meal for a Group

Individuals or organizations that are planning to prepare a nutritionally-sound meal for a group of people should first decide what the nutritional goals of the meal are. Once these goals have been established, the individual or organization should continue the planning process by researching which foods will best satisfy these goals without exceeding the available time and resource limits. The individual or organization should then put together a written meal plan that details what foods will be included, the average time it takes to prepare and cook each of these meals, and the cost associated with the preparation of these meals. Next, they should determine the best method of preparing food for these meals, including which foods should be prepared first, the best way to handle or prepare the foods to minimize the risk of illness, and what techniques can be used to reduce the cooking time. Finally, the individual or organization can prepare the meal according to the plan that has been established.

Reducing the Amount of Time It Takes to Prepare a Meal

Some of the methods that can be used to reduce the time it takes to prepare a meal include keeping the cooking equipment clean and organized, making sure frozen products are thawed ahead of time, preparing foods that have long cooking times beforehand, and preparing foods in order of their cooking times. By keeping the cooking area and the necessary cooking utensils clean, organized, and easily accessible, individuals or organizations can make sure that the time they have available is used as efficiently as possible. Along with thawing products beforehand, preparing foods that require long cooking times ahead of time and re-heating them later can also greatly reduce the amount of time it takes to prepare a meal. As noted, preparing foods according to their cooking times, from longest to shortest, also greatly reduces preparation time because the individual or organization can prepare other foods for the meal while the foods that take the longest are already cooking.

Choosing What Foods to Prepare for a Meal

An individual or organization that is deciding what foods to prepare for a meal should consider the food's nutritional value, the time it takes to prepare each food, the number of people to be served, and the cost of preparing each food. Each food has its own cooking time and offers different nutrients, so it is important that whoever is preparing the meal chooses to serve foods that satisfy people's nutritional goals without exceeding their time constraints for cooking the meal. Since most individuals or organizations will likely have a budgeted amount of money for the meal, they must consider the number of people to be served and how much each food item costs to prepare. If the cost is too high, some meals may not be practical to serve to large groups of people. For example, if an individual or organization is interested in serving a good source of protein for a meal, steak might be a good option for a small group of people but it would probably be too expensive for a larger group.

Food Found in the Marketplace

The two primary types of food that an individual can find in the marketplace are animal products and plant products. Animal products include any foods that either are a part of an animal or are produced by an animal, such as meat, milk, assorted dairy products, and honey. Plant products are foods that originate from some sort of vegetation and include foods such as fruits, vegetables, syrup, nuts, oils, and rice. It is important for an individual to understand the difference between these two groups, as animal products often have more foodborne illnesses associated with them than do plant products; because of this, there are different methods of storing and preparing each type of food to minimize these risks. Animal products and plant products provide different nutrients that the body requires to continue functioning normally, so a healthy individual would need to eat both animal and plant products to receive enough of the various nutrients they require without the use of vitamin supplements.

Factors That Might Influence What Foods are Available to a Consumer

Some of the major factors that might influence what foods are available to a consumer include the region in which a consumer lives, current weather conditions and seasonal effects, and the demand for a particular type of food. Each geographical region has its own natural resources and different climate, which results in foods unique to the area being more readily available. For example, certain crops that react poorly to sudden temperature drops, such as oranges, are easier to grow in areas that have relatively stable and warm climates. Weather and seasonal conditions also play a large role in whether a particular food is available, as certain foods may not be produced during some times of the year in a particular region, while other crops may die as a result of hurricanes, droughts, and other natural disasters. The demand for a particular type of food can also have a significant impact on the availability of that food. Oftentimes, if the demand for a particular type of food increases suddenly, suppliers may have difficulty in meeting that demand.

Food Distributors

Some of the major types of food distributors a consumer might find in the marketplace are chain supermarkets, independent grocery stores, farmers' markets, restaurants, and local farm stands. Each type of food distribution center has its own distinct advantages and disadvantages. Chain supermarkets are large stores that usually offer a large selection of foods at mid-range prices, but foods are often not as fresh and are sometimes of poorer quality than a consumer might find at a farm stand or farmers' market. Independent grocery stores and farmers markets usually have a smaller selection and are slightly more expensive than chain supermarkets, but many consumers prefer to purchase food from these sources because the food is usually locally grown and more fresh. Even though restaurants are the most expensive distributors of food because the food is prepared by the restaurant for the consumer, many people appreciate the quality and variety of foods a restaurant can offer. Local farm stands frequently offer the freshest, highest-quality foods for the lowest prices, but they are open for shorter periods of time, often seasonally.

Food Consumption Patterns

Food consumption patterns are comprised of an analysis of the eating habits of people belonging to a particular region or area. Food consumption patterns indicate that individuals from different regions have very different diets and therefore receive more or less of certain nutrients than individuals from other regions. Knowing the kinds of nutrients that are common in the everyday diets of individuals native to a particular area is important, as that information allows health care professionals to understand what types of diseases and deficiencies pose a threat to the people who live there. By understanding which diseases and vitamin deficiencies the individuals of a particular area may be suffering from, resources can be allocated for treating and preventing those diseases. Monitoring food consumption patterns also allows researchers to study these patterns and determine the ingredients in certain foods that may be contributing to illnesses that are prevalent in a particular region.

Eating Preferences

Just as every individual is fond of certain foods, her or she will dislike or refuse to eat other types of foods as well. In general, people will find the foods that offer them the most physiological and psychological satisfaction to be the most appealing. Most people who refuse to eat a particular food usually do so for one of four basic reasons: they dislike the taste of the food, the condition of the food, how the food was produced, or they fear that the food will make them ill. Such preferences are important because they serve as one of the body's safety mechanisms to prevent individuals from eating foods that may be contaminated or foods that the individual may be allergic to. In some circumstances, however, an individual's eating preferences may need to be ignored so that the body can receive all of the nutrients it needs.

Protecting Consumers from Unsafe Foods and Help Keeping Food Affordable

A number of government regulations in the United States are intended to protect consumers from unsafe foods and help keep food affordable. Some of the most important regulations include food subsidies, price ceilings, tariffs and import quotas, quality-control inspections, and sanitation regulations. Government regulations can manage and even reduce the price of food in several ways: imposing tariffs on imported foods, limiting the amounts of particular foods that can enter the country, offering American farmers and food production facilities financial incentives, and then limiting how much those subsidized producers can charge for their goods. Ideally, these techniques help keep local food sources in business so that the United States does not have to rely too much on outside food sources. Government regulated quality-control inspections and sanitation regulations, such as the Egg Products Inspection Act, the Federal Meat Inspection Act, and the Sanitary Food Transportation Act, all have the purpose of ensuring that foods are produced, stored, and transported following certain guidelines to prevent the food from being contaminated.

Reducing the Risk of Foodborne Illnesses

Some of the methods that can be used to reduce the risk of foodborne illnesses include thawing food appropriately to prevent the growth of bacteria, storing perishable foods in airtight containers and keeping them refrigerated or frozen, and sanitizing all cooking areas and cooking equipment. Individuals should wash their hands before and after handling raw foods, and they should also wash fruits and vegetables before eating to remove any bacteria and pesticides. In addition, foods, especially meats, should be cooked at a high enough temperature for a long enough period of time to avoid the growth of bacteria that lead to foodborne illnesses. Perishable foods should be stored in temperatures of 40 degrees Fahrenheit or below to prevent the growth of bacteria, and frozen foods should be thawed in the refrigerator rather than left out to thaw at room temperature because bacteria grows most quickly at temperatures between 41 degrees and 140 degrees Fahrenheit.

Cooking Equipment

Some of the factors that a consumer should consider when choosing what cooking equipment to purchase include the materials used in the construction of the cooking equipment, the heat conductivity of the materials used, the energy conservation of the cooking equipment, and how easy the equipment is to use and clean. The materials that are used in the construction of a piece of cooking equipment are important because certain materials conduct heat more effectively, retain heat more efficiently, are more durable, and are less expensive than other materials. Certain materials are also rustproof, stick-resistant, and easy to clean, do not flake, and do not react to certain foods. Both the heat conductivity and energy conservation of a piece of cooking equipment are also relevant because the greater the conductivity of the material used in the construction of the equipment and the more efficiently it can retain the heat, the faster the food will cook. Consumers should also know that some types of cooking equipment are easier to use and clean than others, which can make food preparation and clean-up faster.

Food Irradiation and Shelf Life

Food irradiation is the process of using radioactive materials to disinfect and preserve certain types of food. Shelf life refers to how long food will last before it spoils and begins to breed bacteria. Irradiation is important for food manufacturers because it allows a facility to use varying amounts of radiation to kill any bacteria that might be growing on a particular food item, thereby reducing a consumer's risk of foodborne illness. As a result of irradiation techniques that prevent or slow the growth of bacteria, the shelf life of many foods is significantly lengthened. Studies have shown that irradiation methods are completely safe and pose no noticeable risk to individuals who eat foods that have been treated. Foods that are commonly irradiated include apples, bananas, fish, onions, poultry, potatoes, red meats, and strawberries.

Food Preparation

Menu planning is the first step. The menu is the food service's marketing and planning tool to ensure profit. It takes advantage of seasonal and locally-grown food to keep costs under control, and it includes items that can be prepared without excessive time and labor.

Menu specifications are developed so that exactly the right amount of food is purchased. Standardized recipes result in food items being consistent. They also help managers develop work schedules for the kitchen staff.

Foods are cooked by dry heat, moist heat, frying, or a combination of the three. Foods can also be simmered in broth or stock. Appropriate seasonings are used. Foods are portioned using a portion scale. If the food is not served immediately, then proper holding or storage techniques are used to avoid bacteria growth.

The Hazard Analysis Critical Control Point (HACCP) is followed to prevent food-borne illness. It follows the food from purchasing through serving.

Food Presentation

Customers like to see attractively prepared meals served to them; they become eager to eat. The plate needs to be balanced, nicely garnished, and well arranged. Color, shape, arrangement, and texture all influence a diner's appetite. Potatoes, pasta, and rice can be livened up with herbs sprinkled on top. Many food service facilities opt for neutral dishware so that a diner's attention is drawn to the food, not to designs on the rim of the plate.

When plating the food, grease and moisture must be wiped away. An appetizing picture should be created, with garnishes added to provide contrast. Garnishes can also be added to beverages. Food items should be separated from each other. When foods are served on hot plates, customers should be warned by the server so they will not touch the plate and get burned.

Etiquette and Table Service Appropriate for Specific Occasions

Different food operations have different styles. A fast food chain will offer its customers a different atmosphere than an expensive, up-scale operation will offer, and the servers will perform differently. The concept follows from what the food service operation is and what it has on its menu, and this includes types of food, service, price, target market, and theme.

Types of service in the food service industry include counter service, where a customer orders and receives food at a counter before taking it to a table. At a cafeteria service, customers select food from a serving line with a number of choices and serve themselves. A buffet service is similar, except customers receive assistance at an omelet or meat carving station.

Seated service operations seat customers at a table where orders are taken and served by servers. At a banquet service a set menu is served to a group of customers, similar to a catered event.

USDA Dietary Guidelines

The United States Department of Agriculture began issuing nutrition guidelines in 1894, and in 1943 the department began promoting the Basic 7 food groups. In 1956, Basic 7 was replaced with the Basic Four food groups. These were fruits and vegetables, cereals and breads, milk, and meat. Basic Four lasted until 1992, when it was replaced with the Food Pyramid, which divided food into six groups:

1. Bread, cereal, rice, pasta
2. Fruit
3. Vegetables
4. Meat, poultry, fish, dry beans, eggs, nuts
5. Milk, yogurt, cheese
6. Fats, oils, sweets

The Food Pyramid also provided recommendations for the number of daily servings from each group. In 2011, the Food Pyramid was replaced with MyPlate, which used a plate image to show fruits, vegetables, grains, protein, and dairy in a simpler visual format.

The New Pyramid

For the 2025-2030 Dietary Guidelines for Americans, the federal nutrition guide shifted from MyPlate to realfood.gov's New Pyramid. Unlike MyPlate, which focused mainly on dividing a meal into food groups, The New Pyramid emphasizes eating real, whole foods dense in nutrients. Its central message is to get people to choose foods in their natural or minimally processed forms, including protein, dairy, vegetables, fruits, healthy fats, and whole grains. The New Pyramid also encourages people to limit their intake of highly processed foods, refined carbohydrates, added sugars, sugary drinks, excess sodium, unhealthy fats, and artificial ingredients. This change reflects a much broader approach to healthy eating. Instead of focusing solely on portions or food groups, The New Pyramid focuses on the quality of food and encourages people to build meals around foods that provide essential nutrients and support lifelong health.

Chapter Quiz

Ready to see how well you retained what you just read? Scan the QR code to go directly to the chapter quiz interface for this study guide. If you're using a computer, simply visit the online resources page at **mometrix.com/resources719/texesfcshnds** and click the Chapter Quizzes link.

Food, Lodging, and Hospitality

Food, Lodging, and Hospitality Industries

The hospitality industry can be defined as all businesses that serve guests who are away from home. It is composed of two sectors: the lodging industry and the food service industry. Both industries have a pyramid-shaped organizational structure.

At the top of the lodging organization is the general manager. The general manager directs all aspects of the hotel, motel, or resort. Finance, security, and human resource managers report to the general manager. Lower level management personnel are the front desk manager, housekeeping and maintenance managers, and the director of sales. Reporting to these managers are the front desk staff, housekeepers, and security guards.

In the food service industry the general manager directs the operations of all types of restaurants and caterers. Reporting to the general manager are the executive chef, the maître d', and the kitchen steward. These staff persons supervise the cooks, the clean-up staff, hosts/hostesses, wait staff, and bus people.

In the hospitality industry, the product is the goods, services, facilities, and appeal the business provides its customers. Hospitality customers are called "guests;" they expect to be served in a short time, whether it is getting into a room or eating a meal. The adage "the customer is always right" should always be followed. In the lodging industry, rooms should be cleaned and neatened so that the guest feels at home. The front desk staff must be friendly and courteous.

In the food service industry, meals should be prepared attractively, with color provided by fruits, vegetables, and garnishes. The chef should try to create an appetizing picture with the plating of the food. Servers must treat the customer like a special guest. In fast food establishments, serving food warm is more important.

Lodgings and eating establishments must take all precautions to ensure that everything is sanitized to protect customers from bacteria or viral infection. Any such outbreaks can have legal as well as public relations consequences. Food should be stored and prepared properly so that there is a minimum loss of nutrients. There is a current trend toward healthier eating, and people are more aware today of food allergies. This should be considered when planning menus.

Hospitality facilities should take adequate measures to prevent possible injuries to customers, and they should have contingency plans for handling emergencies. Employees must know their individual duties in case of fire. Regular fire drills should be held.

Sanitation Issues and Environmental Protection

Customers expect sanitation in food service and lodging establishments. Such establishments must comply with all health codes. Mildew can form in bathrooms. Illness can result from an improper pH level in a swimming pool. Food-borne illnesses need to be prevented by proper hygiene of employees.

In these industries, there is growing awareness of the environment. The hospitality industry is seen as being a heavy user of resources, as it uses a large amount of water and generates substantial waste. This leads to trends such as landscaping with plants that do not require much water and using recycled paper products. Guests in hotels are now given the option of hanging towels to dry instead of having towels laundered after each use.

Customers demand sanitary conditions in lodging and food service businesses. Employees in food service and lodging establishments must follow all sanitation procedures and should practice good personal hygiene. The businesses must comply with all health codes. Training should be given on how to make surfaces sanitary and prevent mildew from forming in bathrooms. Testing pH levels in swimming pools is important. Kitchen equipment must be cleaned frequently.

Maintenance workers need to be taught landscaping with plants that do not require much water and to use products that will not adversely affect the environment. In lodging facilities, housekeepers can notify guests that they now have the option of hanging towels to dry instead of having towels laundered after each use. Food service workers should be trained on using the **Hazard Analysis Control Point Model** (HACCP) to prevent food-borne illnesses.

Management

The general manager supervises the entire food service or lodging operation and its employees and regularly checks with the managers they oversee to make sure everything is running smoothly. When employee performance excels, then customer satisfaction is high. Competition is stiff in the hospitality industry. Guests can simply go to another hotel or restaurant. Thus, management must continually strive to improve the operation.

There are four styles of management: bureaucratic, democratic, autocratic, and spectator. A good general manager knows when and with whom to use which style. To be a successful manager, a person needs good communication and leadership skills, as well as the ability to perform many tasks at the same time. A manager needs to be good at training and up to date with technology.

Employment Opportunities

The hospitality industry offers service as its product. It is one of the few employment opportunities where one can start at the bottom and work one's way up to a management level position with hard work. Department of Labor projections indicate a strong growth in the coming years.

Employees fall into two categories: **front of the house** and **back of the house** (i.e., those who are seen by guests and those who are not). Entry-level positions are many and include server, bell person, housekeeper, dishwasher, and front desk clerk. Positions requiring some training would include bell captain, concierge, and executive steward. Those requiring a college education include executive chef, front office manager, executive housekeeper, and public relations director. These are just a few of the many opportunities available. Training is possible through job site training, continuing education, and independent study. Grants and scholarships are also available.

Entrepreneurial Opportunities

An **entrepreneur** is someone who starts a new business and who organizes and manages it, taking the associated risks. In the hospitality industry, there are many small businesses that employ fewer than 10 employees, including small boutique hotels, inns, bed and breakfasts, and restaurants.

Entrepreneurs might choose the name, logo, advertising, décor and menus, do the cooking, and clean the rooms. Alternatively, they might decide to buy a franchise, which offers more support and management guidelines with a name that is already known. Most entrepreneurs start small, but those planning to start on a larger scale will most likely need a bank loan and should gain experience in the industry by working for a large facility to start.

Public Policy

The **Occupational Safety and Health Act of 1970** (OSHA) requires businesses to make the workplace free of hazards that could cause injury or death to employees. Compliance officers inspect businesses to ensure that there are no hazards; if any are found, they must be corrected.

OSHA also requires businesses to keep records of all employment-related accidents and to display posters listing the legal rights of employees. If chemicals are handled, Safety Data Sheets (SDS) must be kept on file with details on safe handling and first aid.

The Americans with Disabilities Act of 1992 (ADA) requires that public facilities be accessible fully to disabled persons. Wheelchair ramps, automatic doors, restrooms that are wheelchair accessible, and Braille signs on doors are just a few of the requirements.

Review Video: Intro to OSHA
Visit mometrix.com/academy and enter code: 913559

Industry Standards

A standard of ethics and professionalism is important because hospitality's main purpose is to serve others. A code of ethics should provide specific guidelines for behavior that is morally right and that requires truthfulness in specific situations and applies to all employees. Management should make sure the employees are fully aware of the code and the consequences of not following it.

Theft is a problem in the industry. Employees are exposed to large amounts of cash and credit cards; they see jewelry in people's rooms, place valuables in a safe, and work around large supplies of food and other materials. Kickbacks might be offered by suppliers. Employees might be given bribes to keep an incident secret. Management can minimize these problems by careful screening and background checks of prospective employees and by taking strict action when employees display a breach in the ethics code.

Review Video: Ethical and Professional Standards
Visit mometrix.com/academy and enter code: 391843

Job-Related Competencies and Skills

Having good communication skills is of utmost importance. Getting your ideas across and understanding others is basic. Much communication is by telephone. Proper tone of voice on the phone, pronunciation, and pitch are important to give the right impression. Listening is important, both to guests and co-workers. It involves understanding what is heard and not just daydreaming while someone is talking. Hospitality employees need to have patience, tact, and diplomacy when interacting with guests. They should always be positive and cheerful. They should be attentive to the needs of customers and remember that "the customer is always right." Employees should maintain a professional appearance and be well groomed. Being a team player with fellow workers is important, and computer skills are essential in today's world.

Marketing Techniques

Hospitality businesses have to set goals through marketing plans so they can attract customers, remain profitable, and compete in the market. Even if the business is part of a large corporation or a franchise, it needs to reach its own local market. The plan is a road map used to help sell its services or products and is vital to the success of any business.

A marketing plan helps businesses attract customers away from the competition by persuading them they can better meet the needs and desires of those customers. Using a technique known as positioning, the business paints a specific image of itself that distinguishes it from other businesses. Then the business needs to decide how it is going to communicate its product (through TV, magazines, Internet, etc.).

In the end, marketing helps the business define who its customers are, what they need, and what they want.

Public Relations Techniques

Public relations is communication for the purpose of influencing opinion and promoting a specific image. Publicity received from a public relations release that is presented in the media will benefit the business by drawing attention to it in the community.

There are many occasions where publicity can benefit the business. Rooms or meals could be donated to a local nonprofit agency or charity. The generosity would impress the public when people hear about it. Similarly, a special event that people are interested in might occur at the business.

Public relations keeps the business name familiar to people in the area. Community members are reminded that the business is interested in them. A publicity release about sponsoring a local Little League, for example, provides great public relations and may give more benefit than an advertising campaign.

Quality Assurance

Guestology is the study of guests' needs, wants, and expectations. Lodging guests expect a clean, sanitary room with a comfortable bed. They expect recognition as a guest and want access to laundry and dry cleaning services. They look for information about the city and special events. They like having transportation available.

Guests like having toiletries available if they forgot to pack something. Employees can help by making guests feel important and welcome, and by offering assistance.

Food service customers are hungry and thirsty. They want attention. They want a comfortable and sanitary environment. Customers want the server to remain attentive to their needs. Increasingly, they want healthy food, low in fat and sodium. In general, customers also want variety.

Health Procedures

If a customer is seen to be in need of medical attention, then the front desk manager in a lodging facility or the general manager in a food service operation should be called immediately, and that person should call 911. The manager should then remain with the customer, reassuring the customer that help is on the way and keeping other people away.

If the victim is taken to the hospital by emergency personnel, their belongings will have to be put away for safe keeping until further instructions are received. Asking how to be of assistance in an emergency is consoling and can make the situation easier.

Choking can occur unexpectedly. There should be someone on staff who can administer the Heimlich maneuver to dislodge the object. First aid kits should be maintained to deal with burns, cuts and bruises, and shock, and employees should be trained in how to use them.

Safety Procedures

Employees in the hospitality industry should observe all safety procedures, report any hazards that could cause an accident, and know the location of emergency equipment and how to use it. If the building needs to be evacuated, employees need to know all evacuation routes.

Fire emergencies happen very quickly. A lodging or food service business should have emergency plans that detail employee responsibilities. Emergency meeting locations should be established, and regular emergency drills should be conducted. Employees should be trained in using the proper fire extinguishers and other equipment based on the type of fire. Some employees should be trained to perform CPR.

Procedures should also be established for dealing with weather emergencies and power outages. Employees should be trained on how to avoid panic if any kind of emergency happens.

Supplies

Food service establishments use universal food products (common, everyday products that are always readily available), as well as seasonal and hard-to-get products. Convenience foods that are partially prepared are increasingly being used. Spices, herbs, extracts, and condiments are kept in supply. Baked products are either purchased or made on premises.

Vegetables and fruits are ordered in smaller quantities to avoid spoilage. Various types of salad greens are needed. Gelatin is used to make salads and as a thickener. Many kinds of beverages are supplied, including water, coffee, tea, sodas, and alcoholic beverages.

Lodging and food service operations also both need to have cleaning and sterilizing supplies in stock, as well as bathroom supplies.

Tools

Tools are hand-held equipment used in preparing and serving food. Measuring cups and spoons are used to ensure quality through careful measuring. Thermometers are used to measure the temperature of food; thermometer varieties are confectionary, meat, deep-fat, and dial thermometers. Cutting tools include knives of many different shapes and uses, blade peelers, graters, utility shears, and specialized cutters used for cheese, eggs, tomatoes, and potatoes.

Food handling tools are used for stirring, turning or blending food while cooking, and for serving food in portions. Ladles, scoops, tongs, slotted, perforated and solid spoons, and whisks are commonly used. Rotary beaters are used for beating eggs or batter.

Many kinds of brushes are found in food service facilities. They are used for cleaning food and utensils. Bakers use sifters, pastry blenders, rolling pins, and dough scrapers. Pastry bags are used to apply icing, and pastry wheels cut the dough.

Equipment

Equipment is used for weighing ingredients, opening cans, cutting foods, mixing foods, and cooking food, as well as making and dispensing beverages. Scales are used to save time and ensure accuracy of recipes. Commercial can openers can open everything from small to large institutional size cans. Cutting equipment includes food slicers, vertical food cutters, food processors, and vegetable peelers.

Mixers can be mounted on the floor, bench, or table, with attachments for different ingredients. Blenders are used for high-speed mixing and blending. Beverage equipment includes equipment for making and dispensing coffee, tea, and cold beverages, as well as ice-making machines.

Foods are cooked on grills, range tops, broilers and ovens, and deep-fat fryers. Foods can be steamed or microwaved. New impingement ovens are faster and can make for tastier food. Employees always need to use safety precautions when using and cleaning equipment.

Other Technologies

Up until recently it was very time consuming to make reservations for lodging or dining out. Now, consumers can easily and quickly make online reservations. Computers are used for faster check in and check out.

Key cards are used for entry to rooms, providing extra security. Room TV access was once limited to a few local channels. Now satellite TV provides hundreds of channels and 24-hour news. Rooms are equipped with data ports or wireless access for laptop computers. Employees use computers to clock in and out, and payrolls are electronically deposited. Managers use software programs to make their work more efficient.

Food service servers enter orders using touch screens. Recipes are stored on in-house databases. New advances like cook-chill equipment (which allows food to be prepared in advance and then stored at temperatures just above freezing) provide better-tasting food than frozen food, and they also save time.

Lodging Liability

If a lodging facility refuses to accept or serve a guest, in so doing it might commit a criminal offense that can be punishable by fine or jail term. However, a lodging facility can refuse service to a guest if there are no rooms available, or if the guest is a difficult character, or if the guest is not able to pay for a room. The facility must be able to prove that the guest was exhibiting unfit behavior.

Because a facility is responsible for protecting all its guests, it can refuse to serve a guest who might pose a danger. When a guest becomes ill, the lodging facility is responsible for contacting a physician. If a guest stays longer than originally stated, the guest can be notified that the room has been taken by another guest and arrange for another room. The facility is responsible for guests' personal property up to a posted limit of liability.

Court-Mandated Lodging Security Standards

Court cases have established security standards for the lodging industry. A lodging facility must install adequate locking systems that provide ample security. Public areas and hallways should be well lit. Access to guest areas must be controlled to exclude unauthorized persons.

Monitoring and surveillance systems must be installed in public areas. Adequately trained security personnel should regularly patrol the facility. Staff should be trained in procedures for reporting and dealing with any criminal activity that might occur.

A system for informing guests of any activity around the facility or in the immediate neighborhood that might endanger them should be established and all staff should be trained in advising guests of such activity, as well as when to call for police intervention.

Safety Codes and Laws

There are laws and codes to ensure the safety of guests in lodging facilities. These include laws and codes that mandate fire escape stairways or ladders, fire extinguishers, and smoke detectors in rooms and hallways. There should be well-marked, lighted signs indicating exits and escape routes. Signs in banquet rooms or public spaces must indicate the maximum number of people allowed, so as to allow for safe and orderly evacuation in case of fire.

Fire escape routes must be posted conspicuously in each room. Security bars on windows must have a safety release so they can be opened from the inside to allow egress in an emergency. Laws also mandate a safe water supply for the facility and properly functioning plumbing and ice machines that are available for guests. Elevators are to be inspected regularly. Rooms must be cleaned and sanitized after each use, with clean linens provided.

Accommodating Guests with Disabilities

The Americans with Disabilities Act (ADA) was passed in 1992. It requires that public facilities be open and accessible to people with disabilities. Existing buildings were to be modified by adding wheelchair ramps, automatic doors, wheelchair lifts, wheelchair accessible restrooms, wider parking spaces, guest room numbers in Braille, closed captioning on televisions, and numerous other accommodations.

Facilities that do not comply can be sued for damages by disabled persons. The resulting bad publicity that could result from a lawsuit is usually enough to encourage compliance. Newer facilities use the principles of Universal Design, such as putting entrances at ground level instead of using ramps, having all entrance doors be automatic opening and wide, installing cabinets with shelves that pull out, and light switches with flat panels rather than toggle switches, to name a few.

Legal Expectations of Customers

Facilities that serve customers should admit the customers, operate the business in such a way that customers are not harmed, and sell products and services in an appropriate manner. They have a legal right to refuse admittance to or remove any customer who is a threat or annoyance to other customers or employees.

Food and beverage facilities give customers an implied warranty or unspoken guarantee that their products are fit for human consumption. If unfit, the facility is liable and the customer can be compensated for any damages they might have suffered. The customer must prove that an illness or injury was caused by the food or beverage.

The laws concerning alcohol consumption vary from state to state; however, some activities (such as selling alcohol to a minor or to someone already intoxicated) carry stiff penalties.

Liability in the Food and Lodging Industry with Respect to Employees

Owners, managers, and employees are all responsible for ensuring that their facility complies with all local, state, and federal laws. Workers' Compensation is insurance that pays employees who are injured or become disabled while on the job. Employees cannot sue their employer if injured. A written record must be kept on file of all accidents.

The Occupational Safety and Health Administration (OSHA) is a government agency that enforces safety regulations in the workplace. Employees should report conditions that are unsafe to their supervisors. OSHA compliance officers visit businesses on a regular basis to make sure there are no violations.

Safety Data Sheets must be maintained when chemicals are used. They provide information on health hazards and precautions for safe handling, as well as first aid procedures. The Fair Labor Standards Act regulates minimum wages and rules regarding child labor.

New and Emerging Careers

As in all businesses, there are always changing trends in the food and lodging industry. Because of the ever-increasing presence of computers and smart devices in all businesses, those seeking a career in the hospitality industry should be sure to have a solid knowledge of computer systems and software programs used in the industry.

Certain trends in the hospitality industry indicate that career seekers should get additional training in the fields of adventure tourism and ecotourism, since these types of traveling are extremely popular now. Understanding Universal Design principles would be useful as well. Grounds maintenance is becoming "greener" or more environmentally friendly, and recipes are becoming more health-conscious, so more employees with a background in these fields will be needed.

Retired people are traveling more than in previous generations. Those with a background in geriatric care will be much in demand. Another trend is toward having front desk people who are skilled in more than one language.

Communication Skills

It is important to be able to communicate successfully with guests and co-workers, both verbally and in writing, as well as via electronic communication. Successful employees will project sincerity and courtesy when dealing with guests. One needs to learn when to listen and when to speak, and when to refer a guest to another employee.

Telephone communication skills are very important in the industry, as much of the day-to-day business may be done over the phone. Proper tone of voice and correct pronunciation are necessary. Callers expect to receive information promptly. Having pen and paper at hand allows the employee to write down names, messages, and other important information, and many places have a computer system for data entry. Try to avoid putting callers on hold.

Learning to be a good listener improves relationships with guests and other workers. It is important not to daydream while in conversation. Concentrate on the person who is speaking. When speaking with guests personally, learn to use appropriate body language.

Work Ethics

Set good work habits. Be on time to work. Show a supervisor a willingness to learn new tasks, and complete tasks on time or ahead of time. Personal neatness and cleanliness are important. Be a team player; cooperate with and help other employees. Exhibit a positive attitude in the workplace.

It is important to be able to follow directions. Pay attention to details. If unsure, it is better to ask questions than to perform a task incorrectly. Realize that criticism from a supervisor is meant to improve performance, not to hurt feelings. When an assigned task is complete, look for another job, or offer to help a co-worker.

There will always be situations when problems occur. Learn to remain calm and pause before doing or saying anything to guests, other workers, or supervisors.

Work Habits

Use equipment of any kind carefully and with respect. Show your supervisor and co-workers that you are enthusiastic about your work and truly enjoy what you are doing. Concentrate and avoid getting distracted. Show a willingness to learn new and more efficient techniques. Make sure work meets the standards of the particular business. Remember that the guest is always right and be courteous and polite at all times.

Be willing to do whatever job is assigned to you. Learn the rules and policies of the place of employment and follow them every day. Learn to show initiative and to see what needs to be done without being told. Realize that success comes only with hard work. Learn to work under pressure without becoming inefficient or losing your temper. If unable to go to work, call in as early as possible.

Food Service Skills

Customers evaluate a food operation from the moment they walk in until they leave. All customers must be greeted warmly on arrival. Service should be commensurate with the type of operation. Some food operations emphasize fast food, and a menu should be offered immediately. At a diner or coffee shop, customers are more relaxed. At a formal operation, a customer is presented an open menu by a maître d'.

When taking orders, servers should not be slouched over. Servers can "upsell" the menu by informing customers of the specials of the day. Any questions should be answered politely. The order should be taken according to the policies of the operation. Guests should be asked specifics, such as regarding the preparation of eggs or whether guests desire a cup or bowl of soup.

Food and beverages should be assembled and served according to the type of operation. Hot foods should be taken immediately to customers.

Table Settings

Tables should be covered with correctly-sized tablecloths that do not extend below chair level. When place mats are used, they should be at the edge of the table. Table setting, or cover, depends on the type of operation. The cover usually consists of flatware, dinnerware, glassware, and linens. Cover should be set neatly, since it is a customer's first impression when seated.

Napkins are folded and placed to the left of the fork, or folded and placed in the center of the cover. Forks are placed on the left side of the cover with tines facing up. Knives are on the right side of the table cover, with spoons to the right of the knives.

The placement of glassware depends on the type of operation. Glasses are put on the right side. Bread and butter plates go on the left side. Salad plates are below the bread and butter.

Food Service Techniques in Institutional Settings

Institutional food service serves a captive audience. It can be found in schools, hospitals, correctional facilities, nursing homes, and other facilities. It can be a central commissary, an institutional feeding unit, or an in-plant feeding unit.

A central commissary prepares food in a central kitchen and delivers it to serving locations. Airlines, catering trucks, and some schools use this system. Institutional units prepare and serve food at the same facility. In-plant feeding units provide food for employees in places where other types of food service are not available, such as factories.

An institutional food service can be self-operated or contract-managed. An example of a self-operated unit is a hospital in which the responsibility of management and operation of the food service lie with the hospital. Alternatively, the hospital could choose to hire another company to manage and operate the food service operation.

Customer and Guest Service Practices

Service includes tasks performed for the benefit of guests and customers, as well as types of contact the guest has with the business. Service includes things like checking a guest into a hotel or serving a meal; it also includes greeting a guest with a big smile or helping a customer on the phone.

Guests expect to be served in a short time. They like attention and to feel that they are special during lodging or dining experience. The paramount rule in guest and customer service is "the customer is always right." All employees, from the manager to the housekeeper and from the bus person to the chef, are responsible for providing service.

Lodging guests want a clean, comfortable room. Food service customers want an enjoyable meal in a comfortable setting. Making customers happy results in good word-of-mouth advertising for the operation.

Development and Design

As a result of the Americans with Disabilities Act of 1992 (ADA), hospitality facilities are developed and designed with Universal Design features, which provide the same means of use for everybody, no matter what the disability, without the need for specialization.

Universal Design follows the principle that if it works better for those with disabilities, it works better for everyone. Additionally, with a growing population of elderly persons, it makes life easier for the "baby boomers." It includes wider doors that open automatically, flat entrances, and pull-down cabinets. Universally Designed systems are simple to use and easy to understand and require less physical effort. They have been adopted by hospitality facilities to increase market share and include customers who might have been otherwise passed over.

Maintenance

Maintenance and care of hospitality property means guests are satisfied, business operates smoothly, and equipment investment is protected. Kitchen equipment is exposed to grease, dirt, and food build-up, and must be cleaned frequently for fire prevention and sanitation safety.

Plumbing problems result from normal wear and tear, and systems need to be maintained to prevent damage and waste from leaking pipes. Mildew can be a hazard in bathrooms and kitchens and needs to be treated to prevent disease. All areas need to be treated for insects on a regular basis.

Heating, air conditioning, and refrigeration equipment need to be regularly checked for refrigerant levels and motor condition. They must also be kept clean to run efficiently. Swimming pools need to be checked daily for chlorine and pH levels. Regular landscaping ensures a neat appearance to attract customers. Parking lots have to be repaired of cracks caused by weather and traffic.

Responsibilities of Employees, Supervisors, and Managers

Everyone in the hospitality industry focuses on meeting guests' needs. Customers expect professional service. General managers need to make sure the facility conforms to all health and safety regulations; they develop a management plan and delegate authority to the managers below them to oversee their departments. They also strive to hire employees who project a professional appearance even though they might be young and new to the business.

Supervisors directly oversee employees. They assign tasks according to the area they supervise. If a task is not completed correctly, they must show the employee what was wrong and how to correct it. Both supervisors and employees can be front of the house (meaning they interact with guests, as a front office clerk does), or back of the house (meaning they are usually not seen by guests, as an engineering supervisor is not).

Chapter Quiz

Ready to see how well you retained what you just read? Scan the QR code to go directly to the chapter quiz interface for this study guide. If you're using a computer, simply visit the online resources page at **mometrix.com/resources719/texesfcshnds** and click the Chapter Quizzes link.

TExES Practice Test

Want to take this practice test in an online interactive format?
Check out the online resources page, which includes interactive practice questions and much more: **mometrix.com/resources719/texesfcshnds**

Integration of Foundations

1. A needs assessment for a family and consumer science program should begin with

a. a gap analysis.
b. lesson plans.
c. prioritization.
d. time management analysis.
e. a survey of summative assessment results.

2. Which of the following is NOT a necessary component of an effective syllabus?

a. Grading scale
b. Mission statement
c. List of community resources
d. Clear assessment objectives
e. Course content

3. A lesson plan calls for students to act out a negotiating scenario in which pairs of students try to settle a hypothetical dispute between a husband and wife over money. Which learning disability might prevent a student from succeeding at this task?

a. Dyssemia
b. Apraxia
c. Dysgraphia
d. Dyslexia
e. Visual perception disorder

4. When evaluating Internet research, what is the least important consideration?

a. Whether the website has an editorial board
b. The organization that maintains the website
c. The presence of links to similar websites
d. The last time the website was updated
e. An affiliation with the United States government

5. Many high-school students believe that the most important content area in family and consumer science is

a. housing.
b. the family.
c. consumer science.
d. personal finance.
e. food and nutrition.

6. The original purpose of family and consumer science education was to

a. redress social problems such as child labor and the repression of women.
b. improve women's housekeeping skills.
c. encourage frugality during the World War II.
d. reinforce traditional family roles.
e. encourage the use of household appliances.

7. Which of the following activities would best develop the psychomotor skills of elementary-school students?

a. Learning to calculate compound interest
b. Creating a budget for their school wardrobe
c. Looking up banking terms in the dictionary
d. Setting up a mock storefront for a retail business
e. Drawing a picture of their ideal house

8. Name one advantage of large classes.

a. Close relations between students and teacher
b. Greater access to resources
c. Expanded range of teaching methods
d. Less record-keeping
e. Greater comfort for the teacher

9. Which of the following is NOT a relevant factor when making changes in the family and consumer sciences curriculum?

a. Experience
b. Knowledge
c. Time
d. Skill
e. Expense

10. A teacher is dividing the class up into groups for a project. What is the best way to avoid gender discrimination?

a. Segregate the groups by gender.
b. Encourage boys to include girls when making decisions.
c. Encourage girls to handle tasks related to math.
d. Be sure each group is comprised of both boys and girls.
e. Give leadership positions to at least one boy and one girl in each group.

11. The primary determinant of whether a teacher will adopt instructional technology is

a. estimated cost.
b. student interest.
c. perceived usefulness.
d. the teacher's aptitude.
e. geographic location.

12. The Carl D. Perkins Improvement Act of 2006 mandated that

a. children with disabilities be given a free lunch.
b. the curriculum of family and consumer science be aligned with general content standards.
c. family and consumer science teachers obtain an undergraduate degree.
d. students in family and consumer sciences pass a written examination.
e. family and consumer sciences teachers focus on career training.

13. An activity that requires students to describe their ideal home falls within the

a. psychomotor domain.
b. analytic domain.
c. cognitive domain.
d. affective domain.
e. synthetic domain.

14. Children between the ages of six and eight should be able to

a. make change.
b. compare the prices of products.
c. maintain spending records.
d. use the terminology associated with banking.
e. count coins.

Nutrition, Wellness, and Food Service

15. What is the major benefit of vitamin A?

a. It helps form new cells.
b. It helps protect the body from disease.
c. It can increase a person's concentration and alertness.
d. It can give a person healthy hair and skin.
e. It enables muscle contraction.

16. Which food group has a recommended daily intake of two and half cups?

a. Grains
b. Dairy
c. Fruits
d. Vegetables
e. Protein foods

17. The daily values listed on food packaging assume that

a. the food will be shared between two people.
b. the food will not be cooked.
c. a person's daily diet consists of two thousand calories.
d. the product contains preservatives.
e. the product is unspoiled.

18. In order to reduce the risk of spinal bifida in infants, food manufacturers have begun adding

a. calcium.
b. folic acid.
c. iron.
d. vitamin K.
e. magnesium.

19. Which of the following events decreases metabolism?

a. Rapid weight loss
b. Increase in muscle mass
c. Slow weight gain
d. Moderate workout
e. Rapid weight gain

20. An ovo-lacto-vegetarian is a person who eats

a. Fruits, vegetables, and grains
b. Fruits, vegetables, grains, and poultry
c. Fruits, vegetables, grains, and dairy products
d. Fruits, vegetables, grains, dairy products, and eggs
e. Fruits, vegetables, grains, and eggs

21. Sodium and chloride are major minerals; every day a person should consume ____________ of each.

a. 100 milligrams
b. 1 kilogram
c. 10 milligrams
d. 10 grams
e. 1 gram

22. Which of the following vitamins is water-soluble?

a. Vitamin D
b. Vitamin E
c. Vitamin K
d. Vitamin A
e. Vitamin C

23. What is one problem associated with the over-consumption of protein?

a. Dehydration
b. Increased muscle mass
c. Strained liver and kidneys
d. Heart palpitations
e. Dandruff

24. Which kind of oil is NOT an unsaturated fat?

a. Corn oil
b. Olive oil
c. Canola oil
d. Palm oil
e. Sunflower oil

25. The amount of energy required to raise the temperature of one gram of water by one degree Celsius is a(n)

a. joule.
b. calorie.
c. ohm.
d. microgram.
e. watt.

26. A person who is 41 to 100% heavier than his or her ideal weight is

a. mildly obese.
b. osteoporotic.
c. diabetic.
d. moderately obese.
e. severely obese.

27. Which of the following statements is true?

I. Bulimia can lead to tooth decay.
II. Anorexics tend to have a distorted self-image.
III. Bulimia does not always include purging.

a. I only
b. II only
c. III only
d. I and II only
e. I, II, and III

28. Which nutrient is not present in high levels in dairy products?

a. Vitamin B-12
b. Iron
c. Protein
d. Vitamin A
e. Calcium

29. Which of the following vitamins is known to improve the body's ability to use phosphorus and calcium?

a. Vitamin E
b. Vitamin D
c. Vitamin B-3
d. Vitamin K
e. Vitamin A

30. What is one drawback of inpatient treatment for alcoholism?

a. It is rarely effective.
b. It does not include a twelve-step program.
c. It enables the patient to continue drinking while receiving treatment.
d. It is expensive.
e. It requires a personal commitment from the patient.

Answer Key and Explanations

Integration of Foundations

1. A: A needs assessment for a family and consumer science program should begin with a gap analysis, in which the performance of the class is compared to the performance of students at leading schools. While this may involve a survey of summative assessment results, it should also include a look at the instructional methods, equipment, and community support at the respective schools. This process is similar to the benchmarking performed by business leaders, wherein a business is compared to its most successful competitor. The idea is to bring one's own performance in line with the top performer in one's field. The subsequent needs analysis will define the ways in which the family and consumer science program should improve its approach to leaders in the field.

2. C: A list of community resources is not one of the necessary components of an effective syllabus. A syllabus is essential for organizing the structure and content of a family and consumer science class. Many students do not know what such a course entails, so the syllabus should include a clear mission statement and outline of the course content. The mission statement should state the specific goals of the class. The syllabus should also include clear assessment objectives and an explanation of the grading scale to be used. Experienced teachers know that making the assessment and grading protocols explicit at the beginning of the year can eliminate a great deal of trouble later on.

3. A: Dyssemia is a learning disability that might prevent a student from succeeding in a role-play activity. Dyssemia is a disorder which makes it hard to distinguish social cues and signals. A student with this problem would have a difficult time interpreting the gestures and underlying emotions of his or her fellow participants. Dyssemic students require special instruction about reading another person's body language and vocal tone. Apraxia is a learning disability that inhibits the ability to coordinate movements to accomplish a particular goal. Dysgraphia is associated with difficulty in writing and spelling. Dyslexia is a broad category of language-related learning disabilities that extend beyond reading. Visual perception disorders make it hard for students to identify written words and symbols.

4. E: Of the given factors, an affiliation with the United States government is the least important consideration in the evaluation of Internet research. There are a number of federal government websites that can be valuable for a family and consumer science teacher, but this affiliation is not a guarantee of utility. The Internet can be a great resource for information about family and consumer science, but an educator must ensure that the information obtained online is accurate and from a reputable source. The other four answer choices are factors that should receive consideration when a person is deciding whether a website is credible. Trustworthy websites, especially those connected with universities and government departments, have an editorial board that approves content. The organization that maintains the website should be easy to discover and investigate. A good website is likely to have links to other, similar websites. Just as we can tell a lot about people by their friends, so we can tell a lot about a site by its links. A trustworthy website will be updated frequently.

5. E: A number of high-school students believe that the most important content area in family and consumer science is food and nutrition. Moreover, this is the most popular family and consumer science subject among high-school students. Perhaps this is because food and nutrition are more relevant to the current lives of high-school students, especially those who are concerned with their physical appearance and health. Housing, family development, and personal finance may not yet be pertinent subjects in the lives of young people. It is incumbent upon the family and consumer sciences teacher, then, to emphasize the importance of these subjects.

6. A: The original purpose of family and consumer science education was to redress social problems such as child labor and the repression of women. In the last years of the nineteenth century, Ellen Swallow Richards convened a group of social reform-minded educators at Lake Placid, New York, to develop programs for domestic economy and household management. These programs were the beginning of what has become family and consumer science education. It is important for teachers to acknowledge that the roots of this subject are in social reform. Even now, the underlying intention of family and consumer science education should be to empower students in their family lives by teaching them to manage their finances and consumer decisions.

7. D: Setting up a mock storefront for a retail business is one way to develop the psychomotor skills of elementary-school students. Psychomotor skills are best acquired through physical action. Setting up a storefront is one such activity, since the best way to learn about product placement is to practice it rather than read or be told about it. Learning to calculate compound interest and looking up banking terms in the dictionary are activities that develop cognitive skills. Drawing a picture of one's ideal house is a good way to develop affective skills. The creation of a budget for a school wardrobe requires a combination of cognitive and affective skills, insofar as the students will need to decide which clothes they want to buy and then work out a comprehensive pricing list.

8. B: One advantage of large classes is that they tend to have greater access to resources. Large classes have more students, and therefore more connections to the community. These connections can be extremely useful in a family and consumer science class. Also, schools are likely to apportion more equipment and financial resources to larger classes. For these reasons, teachers of large classes often have excellent resources at their disposal. The other answer choices are false statements. Large classes tend to create poorer relations between students and teacher, as there are simply too many students for the teacher to establish close relations with each one. Large classes tend to limit the teaching methods that can be used, since some activities are not manageable with a large group. Teachers must keep records for every student, so it stands to reason that larger classes will create more paperwork. Finally, most teachers are more comfortable in an intimate setting with just a few students.

9. A: Experience is not considered a relevant factor when making changes in the family and consumer sciences curriculum. Teachers of all levels of experience should be able to adapt their method and content when called upon to do so. In recent years, there has been pressure for the family and consumer science curriculum to be more closely aligned with general content standards. Teachers do report that knowledge, time, skill, and expense can be significant barriers to change in the curriculum. In particular, many teachers claim that they do not have enough time to implement major changes. The knowledge and skill obstacles may not be the fault of the teacher; for instance, a teacher might not get approval for changes from an administrator who is ignorant about the subject.

10. E: When dividing students up into groups for a project, the best way to avoid gender discrimination is to assign leadership positions to boys and girls in each group. Answer choice D is also a good idea, but it is implicit in answer choice E. Groups should never be segregated by gender unless there is a specific reason for doing so. Also, students should be discouraged from always performing the tasks stereotypically associated with their gender. For example, boys should be encouraged to assume roles related to the arts, while girls should be given opportunities to work with math and science. For most teachers, the best defense against gender discrimination is awareness and a commitment to equal treatment for all students.

11. C: The primary determinant of whether a teacher will adopt instructional technology is perceived usefulness. The cost of the technology is basically irrelevant to the teacher, since it is the school or district that will bear the cost. Student interest is of some importance, since the technology will not be successful unless it is engaging to the students. However, there are plenty of engaging technologies that have little application in the classroom. Geographic location has very little bearing on adoption of technology, since most equipment is available in all parts of the country. Finally, the teacher's aptitude is slightly less important than perceived usefulness, since most teachers assume that they can learn how to use new technologies in a fairly short time.

12. B: The Carl D. Perkins Improvement Act of 2006 mandated that the curriculum of family and consumer science be aligned with general content standards. This act is an offshoot of the No Child Left Behind Act. Its intention is to boost proficiency by ensuring that the content of family and consumer science classes reinforces general academic knowledge. It is part of a general effort to standardize career and technical (formerly known as vocational) education.

13. D: An activity that requires students to describe their ideal home falls within the affective domain. This domain of education encompasses all of the emotional responses to subjects. A child's emotional responses evolve in a manner similar to their intellectual and physical responses. When students are asked to describe his or her ideal house, they are essentially organizing imaginative elements into a coherent response. This management of the imagination is an important skill. The affective domain is one of three outlined in Bloom's taxonomy. The other two are the psychomotor and cognitive domains, concerned with physical and intellectual skills, respectively.

14. E: Between the ages of six and eight, children should develop the ability to count coins. In the first few years of school, children should learn the values of the various coins, and should be able to assemble different combinations of coins to produce the same value. At this age, children should understand the general purpose of a bank and a savings account. Some children at this age will be able to manage a small allowance. All of the other answer choices are more advanced skills. Making change, comparing prices, maintaining records, and using banking terms are skills not typically developed until at least age nine.

Nutrition, Wellness, and Food Service

15. D: The major benefit of vitamin A is that it helps the body produce healthy hair and skin. Carrots, pumpkins, fish, and eggs are all good sources of vitamin A. Help with forming new cells is a major benefit of folate, or folic acid. There is a great deal of folate in spinach and fortified grains. Vitamin C is one of the primary disease-fighting nutrients. It is obtained most effectively from citrus fruits and broccoli. Concentration and alertness are improved by vitamin B-12. It is most abundant in fish, poultry, and eggs. Calcium is a mineral that helps muscles contract. It is abundant in dairy products and sardines.

16. D: The United States Department of Agriculture recommends two and a half cups of vegetables daily. The other recommended amounts are as follows: grains (six ounces); fruits (two cups); dairy (three cups); protein foods (five and a half ounces).

17. C: The recommended daily values listed on food packaging assume a daily diet of two thousand calories. Adult males are generally advised to eat about this many calories every day. Women and children, however, may require fewer calories, while athletes may require more. When one's recommended caloric intake is considerably lower or higher than two thousand, one must make necessary adjustments to the daily values.

18. B: Food manufacturers now add folic acid to their products because it has been shown to reduce the risk of spinal bifida in infants. Folic acid is a B vitamin that aids in the synthesis of hemoglobin, which is required to transport oxygen throughout the bloodstream. Pregnant women, women who are trying to become pregnant, and elderly people should all ensure that their diet includes foods with folic acid. There are also a number of safe supplements containing folic acid.

19. A: Losing weight quickly decreases the metabolism. Nutritionists and doctors believe that this is a form of self-defense by the body, which senses that food is not as available and therefore tries to limit its use of calories. All of the other answer choices are events that increase metabolism. Weight gain always raises metabolism, in part because there is more muscle or fat to provide with nutrients. Muscle burns more calories than fat, so an increase in muscle mass will correlate with an increase in metabolism. Any exercise tends to increase metabolism.

20. D: An ovo-lacto-vegetarian is a person who eats fruits, vegetables, grains, dairy products, and eggs. These people get most of their proteins from beans, eggs, milk, and cheese. There are several other kinds of vegetarians. A vegan is someone who eats only plant foods; vegans do not eat any meat or animal product, including honey. Lacto-vegetarians eat fruits, vegetables, grains, and dairy products.

21. A: A person should consume 100 milligrams of major minerals, including sodium and chloride, every day. Of course, sodium and chloride can both be obtained from table salt. Some of the other major minerals are potassium, calcium, phosphorus, and magnesium. Trace minerals, such as iron, zinc, and copper, need only be consumed at a rate of 10 milligrams every day. The precise effect of these minerals on the body has not yet been determined.

22. E: Vitamin C is water-soluble, meaning that it is absorbed into the blood stream and can be forced out of the body through urine and sweat. For example, caffeinated beverages can increase the urine stream and thereby diminish the absorption of water-soluble nutrients like vitamin C. Vitamin B is another water-soluble nutrient. Other vitamins, including A, D, E, and K, are absorbed by the intestinal membrane; these vitamins are said to be fat-soluble. Vitamin D can also be obtained from sunlight.

23. C: An overconsumption of protein can put strain on the kidneys and liver. This is one reason why doctors discourage the use of body-building supplements and protein shakes unless under medical supervision. An excessive consumption of protein can lead to general imbalances in diet, which can undermine fitness in the long run. Protein does contribute to the development of muscle mass, but this is not necessarily a problem. Weight-lifting and vigorous physical activities require complex carbohydrates as well as proteins.

24. D: Palm oil is not an unsaturated fat. On the contrary, it is a saturated fat, meaning that excessive consumption of it can lead to heart disease. Coconut oil, butter, and lard are some of the other saturated fats. The other answer choices are unsaturated fats, which are better for the body. In fact, olive oil and canola oil can reduce the amount of cholesterol in the body.

25. B: A calorie is the amount of energy required to raise the temperature of one gram of water by one degree Celsius. In the United States, every packaged food must contain a listing of the number of calories per serving. Also, whereas in the past it was possible for manufacturers to confuse the consumer by indicating odd serving sizes, the designation of serving size is now regulated by the federal government. All the manufacturers of a particular product are required to use similar serving sizes.

26. D: A person who is 41 to 100% heavier than his or her ideal weight is moderately obese. Health professionals have divided obesity into three degrees: mild, moderate, and severe. A person who is less than 20% heavier than his or her ideal weight is considered merely overweight, but a person who is 20 to 40% heavier is considered mildly obese. People who are more than 100% heavier than their ideal weight are severely obese. Moderately obese people are much more likely to have diabetes or osteoporosis, but do not necessarily suffer from these conditions.

27. E: All three of the statements are true. Bulimia can lead to tooth decay, due to a combination of malnutrition and corrosion by stomach acid. Anorexics often have a distorted self-image, believing themselves to be much heavier than they actually are. Finally, bulimia does not always include purging (induced vomiting or defecation). Bulimics may obsessively exercise or abstain from food in order to lose weight. Both anorexia and bulimia are extremely dangerous and should be discussed at great length in the nutrition component of a family and consumer science class. These conditions are especially common among middle-school and high-school students.

28. B: Dairy products do not contain significant amounts of iron. The other answer choices, however, are nutrients that are abundant in dairy products. Riboflavin is another nutrient found in great quantities in dairy products. According to the USDA, people should eat two or three servings of dairy every day. A serving is equivalent to eight ounces of milk, a cup of yogurt, or one and a half ounces of cheese. People should be careful about which dairy products they consume, as many contain a great deal of fat.

29. B: Vitamin D is known to help the body absorb the phosphorus and calcium obtained through a person's diet. It is present in small amounts in foods like fish and eggs and is especially present in cod liver oil. Vitamin E is a major antioxidant, meaning that it eliminates cells that can have a deleterious effect on the body. This vitamin is found in good amounts in wheat germ oil, milk, and plant leaves. Vitamin B-3, also known as niacin, helps to reduce levels of cholesterol in the blood. It is found in yeast, dairy products, and wheat germ. Vitamin K promotes blood clotting. It is abundant in spinach, cabbage, and soybeans. Vitamin A contributes to the growth and maintenance of body tissues. It is particularly present in eggs, spinach, and liver.

30. D: One drawback of inpatient treatment for alcoholism is that it is expensive. In addition, inpatient programs are often not covered by health insurance, so the patient and his or her family may be forced to pay out of pocket. The efficacy of these programs is well established, however. Some studies estimate that 70% of the participants in inpatient programs stay sober for at least five years. Many of these inpatient programs include the twelve-step process, most famously represented by Alcoholics Anonymous. Patients cannot continue to drink while they are enrolled in an inpatient program, since they are living on the grounds of the treatment facility. Finally, it is true that inpatient programs require the personal commitment of the patient, but this is true of all rehabilitation programs.

How to Overcome Test Anxiety

Just the thought of taking a test is enough to make most people a little nervous. A test is an important event that can have a long-term impact on your future, so it's important to take it seriously and it's natural to feel anxious about performing well. But just because anxiety is normal, that doesn't mean that it's helpful in test taking, or that you should simply accept it as part of your life. Anxiety can have a variety of effects. These effects can be mild, like making you feel slightly nervous, or severe, like blocking your ability to focus or remember even a simple detail.

If you experience test anxiety—whether severe or mild—it's important to know how to beat it. To discover this, first you need to understand what causes test anxiety.

Causes of Test Anxiety

While we often think of anxiety as an uncontrollable emotional state, it can actually be caused by simple, practical things. One of the most common causes of test anxiety is that a person does not feel adequately prepared for their test. This feeling can be the result of many different issues such as poor study habits or lack of organization, but the most common culprit is time management. Starting to study too late, failing to organize your study time to cover all of the material, or being distracted while you study will mean that you're not well prepared for the test. This may lead to cramming the night before, which will cause you to be physically and mentally exhausted for the test. Poor time management also contributes to feelings of stress, fear, and hopelessness as you realize you are not well prepared but don't know what to do about it.

Other times, test anxiety is not related to your preparation for the test but comes from unresolved fear. This may be a past failure on a test, or poor performance on tests in general. It may come from comparing yourself to others who seem to be performing better or from the stress of living up to expectations. Anxiety may be driven by fears of the future—how failure on this test would affect your educational and career goals. These fears are often completely irrational, but they can still negatively impact your test performance.

Elements of Test Anxiety

As mentioned earlier, test anxiety is considered to be an emotional state, but it has physical and mental components as well. Sometimes you may not even realize that you are suffering from test anxiety until you notice the physical symptoms. These can include trembling hands, rapid heartbeat, sweating, nausea, and tense muscles. Extreme anxiety may lead to fainting or vomiting. Obviously, any of these symptoms can have a negative impact on testing. It is important to recognize them as soon as they begin to occur so that you can address the problem before it damages your performance.

The mental components of test anxiety include trouble focusing and inability to remember learned information. During a test, your mind is on high alert, which can help you recall information and stay focused for an extended period of time. However, anxiety interferes with your mind's natural processes, causing you to blank out, even on the questions you know well. The strain of testing during anxiety makes it difficult to stay focused, especially on a test that may take several hours. Extreme anxiety can take a huge mental toll, making it difficult not only to recall test information but even to understand the test questions or pull your thoughts together.

Effects of Test Anxiety

Test anxiety is like a disease—if left untreated, it will get progressively worse. Anxiety leads to poor performance, and this reinforces the feelings of fear and failure, which in turn lead to poor performances on subsequent tests. It can grow from a mild nervousness to a crippling condition. If allowed to progress, test anxiety can have a big impact on your schooling, and consequently on your future.

Test anxiety can spread to other parts of your life. Anxiety on tests can become anxiety in any stressful situation, and blanking on a test can turn into panicking in a job situation. But fortunately, you don't have to let anxiety rule your testing and determine your grades. There are a number of relatively simple steps you can take to move past anxiety and function normally on a test and in the rest of life.

Physical Steps for Beating Test Anxiety

While test anxiety is a serious problem, the good news is that it can be overcome. It doesn't have to control your ability to think and remember information. While it may take time, you can begin taking steps today to beat anxiety.

Just as your first hint that you may be struggling with anxiety comes from the physical symptoms, the first step to treating it is also physical. Rest is crucial for having a clear, strong mind. If you are tired, it is much easier to give in to anxiety. But if you establish good sleep habits, your body and mind will be ready to perform optimally, without the strain of exhaustion. Additionally, sleeping well helps you to retain information better, so you're more likely to recall the answers when you see the test questions.

Getting good sleep means more than going to bed on time. It's important to allow your brain time to relax. Take study breaks from time to time so it doesn't get overworked, and don't study right before bed. Take time to rest your mind before trying to rest your body, or you may find it difficult to fall asleep.

Along with sleep, other aspects of physical health are important in preparing for a test. Good nutrition is vital for good brain function. Sugary foods and drinks may give a burst of energy but this burst is followed by a crash, both physically and emotionally. Instead, fuel your body with protein and vitamin-rich foods.

Also, drink plenty of water. Dehydration can lead to headaches and exhaustion, especially if your brain is already under stress from the rigors of the test. Particularly if your test is a long one, drink water during the breaks. And if possible, take an energy-boosting snack to eat between sections.

Along with sleep and diet, a third important part of physical health is exercise. Maintaining a steady workout schedule is helpful, but even taking 5-minute study breaks to walk can help get your blood pumping faster and clear your head. Exercise also releases endorphins, which contribute to a positive feeling and can help combat test anxiety.

When you nurture your physical health, you are also contributing to your mental health. If your body is healthy, your mind is much more likely to be healthy as well. So take time to rest, nourish your body with healthy food and water, and get moving as much as possible. Taking these physical steps will make you stronger and more able to take the mental steps necessary to overcome test anxiety.

Mental Steps for Beating Test Anxiety

Working on the mental side of test anxiety can be more challenging, but as with the physical side, there are clear steps you can take to overcome it. As mentioned earlier, test anxiety often stems from lack of preparation, so the obvious solution is to prepare for the test. Effective studying may be the most important weapon you have for beating test anxiety, but you can and should employ several other mental tools to combat fear.

First, boost your confidence by reminding yourself of past success—tests or projects that you aced. If you're putting as much effort into preparing for this test as you did for those, there's no reason you should expect to fail here. Work hard to prepare; then trust your preparation.

Second, surround yourself with encouraging people. It can be helpful to find a study group, but be sure that the people you're around will encourage a positive attitude. If you spend time with others who are anxious or cynical, this will only contribute to your own anxiety. Look for others who are motivated to study hard from a desire to succeed, not from a fear of failure.

Third, reward yourself. A test is physically and mentally tiring, even without anxiety, and it can be helpful to have something to look forward to. Plan an activity following the test, regardless of the outcome, such as going to a movie or getting ice cream.

When you are taking the test, if you find yourself beginning to feel anxious, remind yourself that you know the material. Visualize successfully completing the test. Then take a few deep, relaxing breaths and return to it. Work through the questions carefully but with confidence, knowing that you are capable of succeeding.

Developing a healthy mental approach to test taking will also aid in other areas of life. Test anxiety affects more than just the actual test—it can be damaging to your mental health and even contribute to depression. It's important to beat test anxiety before it becomes a problem for more than testing.

Study Strategy

Being prepared for the test is necessary to combat anxiety, but what does being prepared look like? You may study for hours on end and still not feel prepared. What you need is a strategy for test prep. The next few pages outline our recommended steps to help you plan out and conquer the challenge of preparation.

Step 1: Scope Out the Test

Learn everything you can about the format (multiple choice, essay, etc.) and what will be on the test. Gather any study materials, course outlines, or sample exams that may be available. Not only will this help you to prepare, but knowing what to expect can help to alleviate test anxiety.

Step 2: Map Out the Material

Look through the textbook or study guide and make note of how many chapters or sections it has. Then divide these over the time you have. For example, if a book has 15 chapters and you have five days to study, you need to cover three chapters each day. Even better, if you have the time, leave an extra day at the end for overall review after you have gone through the material in depth.

If time is limited, you may need to prioritize the material. Look through it and make note of which sections you think you already have a good grasp on, and which need review. While you are studying, skim quickly through the familiar sections and take more time on the challenging parts.

Write out your plan so you don't get lost as you go. Having a written plan also helps you feel more in control of the study, so anxiety is less likely to arise from feeling overwhelmed at the amount to cover.

Step 3: Gather Your Tools

Decide what study method works best for you. Do you prefer to highlight in the book as you study and then go back over the highlighted portions? Or do you type out notes of the important information? Or is it helpful to make flashcards that you can carry with you? Assemble the pens, index cards, highlighters, post-it notes, and any other materials you may need so you won't be distracted by getting up to find things while you study.

If you're having a hard time retaining the information or organizing your notes, experiment with different methods. For example, try color-coding by subject with colored pens, highlighters, or post-it notes. If you learn better by hearing, try recording yourself reading your notes so you can listen while in the car, working out, or simply sitting at your desk. Ask a friend to quiz you from your flashcards, or try teaching someone the material to solidify it in your mind.

Step 4: Create Your Environment

It's important to avoid distractions while you study. This includes both the obvious distractions like visitors and the subtle distractions like an uncomfortable chair (or a too-comfortable couch that makes you want to fall asleep). Set up the best study environment possible: good lighting and a comfortable work area. If background music helps you focus, you may want to turn it on, but otherwise keep the room quiet. If you are using a computer to take notes, be sure you don't have any other windows open, especially applications like social media, games, or anything else that could distract you. Silence your phone and turn off notifications. Be sure to keep water close by so you stay hydrated while you study (but avoid unhealthy drinks and snacks).

Also, take into account the best time of day to study. Are you freshest first thing in the morning? Try to set aside some time then to work through the material. Is your mind clearer in the afternoon or evening? Schedule your study session then. Another method is to study at the same time of day that you will take the test, so that your brain gets used to working on the material at that time and will be ready to focus at test time.

Step 5: Study!

Once you have done all the study preparation, it's time to settle into the actual studying. Sit down, take a few moments to settle your mind so you can focus, and begin to follow your study plan. Don't give in to distractions or let yourself procrastinate. This is your time to prepare so you'll be ready to fearlessly approach the test. Make the most of the time and stay focused.

Of course, you don't want to burn out. If you study too long you may find that you're not retaining the information very well. Take regular study breaks. For example, taking five minutes out of every hour to walk briskly, breathing deeply and swinging your arms, can help your mind stay fresh.

As you get to the end of each chapter or section, it's a good idea to do a quick review. Remind yourself of what you learned and work on any difficult parts. When you feel that you've mastered the material, move on to the next part. At the end of your study session, briefly skim through your notes again.

But while review is helpful, cramming last minute is NOT. If at all possible, work ahead so that you won't need to fit all your study into the last day. Cramming overloads your brain with more information than it can process and retain, and your tired mind may struggle to recall even previously learned information when it is overwhelmed with last-minute study. Also, the urgent nature of cramming and the stress placed on your brain contribute to anxiety. You'll be more likely to go to the test feeling unprepared and having trouble thinking clearly.

So don't cram, and don't stay up late before the test, even just to review your notes at a leisurely pace. Your brain needs rest more than it needs to go over the information again. In fact, plan to finish your studies by noon or early afternoon the day before the test. Give your brain the rest of the day to relax or focus on other things, and get a good night's sleep. Then you will be fresh for the test and better able to recall what you've studied.

Step 6: Take a Practice Test

Many courses offer sample tests, either online or in the study materials. This is an excellent resource to check whether you have mastered the material, as well as to prepare for the test format and environment.

Check the test format ahead of time: the number of questions, the type (multiple choice, free response, etc.), and the time limit. Then create a plan for working through them. For example, if you have 30 minutes to take a 60-question test, your limit is 30 seconds per question. Spend less time on the questions you know well so that you can take more time on the difficult ones.

If you have time to take several practice tests, take the first one open book, with no time limit. Work through the questions at your own pace and make sure you fully understand them. Gradually work up to taking a test under test conditions: sit at a desk with all study materials put away and set a timer. Pace yourself to make sure you finish the test with time to spare and go back to check your answers if you have time.

After each test, check your answers. On the questions you missed, be sure you understand why you missed them. Did you misread the question (tests can use tricky wording)? Did you forget the information? Or was it something you hadn't learned? Go back and study any shaky areas that the practice tests reveal.

Taking these tests not only helps with your grade, but also aids in combating test anxiety. If you're already used to the test conditions, you're less likely to worry about it, and working through tests until you're scoring well gives you a confidence boost. Go through the practice tests until you feel comfortable, and then you can go into the test knowing that you're ready for it.

Test Tips

On test day, you should be confident, knowing that you've prepared well and are ready to answer the questions. But aside from preparation, there are several test day strategies you can employ to maximize your performance.

First, as stated before, get a good night's sleep the night before the test (and for several nights before that, if possible). Go into the test with a fresh, alert mind rather than staying up late to study.

Try not to change too much about your normal routine on the day of the test. It's important to eat a nutritious breakfast, but if you normally don't eat breakfast at all, consider eating just a protein bar. If you're a coffee drinker, go ahead and have your normal coffee. Just make sure you time it so that the caffeine doesn't wear off right in the middle of your test. Avoid sugary beverages, and drink enough water to stay hydrated but not so much that you need a restroom break 10 minutes into the test. If your test isn't first thing in the morning, consider going for a walk or doing a light workout before the test to get your blood flowing.

Allow yourself enough time to get ready, and leave for the test with plenty of time to spare so you won't have the anxiety of scrambling to arrive in time. Another reason to be early is to select a good seat. It's helpful to sit away from doors and windows, which can be distracting. Find a good seat, get out your supplies, and settle your mind before the test begins.

When the test begins, start by going over the instructions carefully, even if you already know what to expect. Make sure you avoid any careless mistakes by following the directions.

Then begin working through the questions, pacing yourself as you've practiced. If you're not sure on an answer, don't spend too much time on it, and don't let it shake your confidence. Either skip it and come back later, or eliminate as many wrong answers as possible and guess among the remaining ones. Don't dwell on these questions as you continue—put them out of your mind and focus on what lies ahead.

Be sure to read all of the answer choices, even if you're sure the first one is the right answer. Sometimes you'll find a better one if you keep reading. But don't second-guess yourself if you do immediately know the answer. Your gut instinct is usually right. Don't let test anxiety rob you of the information you know.

If you have time at the end of the test (and if the test format allows), go back and review your answers. Be cautious about changing any, since your first instinct tends to be correct, but make sure you didn't misread any of the questions or accidentally mark the wrong answer choice. Look over any you skipped and make an educated guess.

At the end, leave the test feeling confident. You've done your best, so don't waste time worrying about your performance or wishing you could change anything. Instead, celebrate the successful completion of this test. And finally, use this test to learn how to deal with anxiety even better next time.

Review Video: Test Anxiety
Visit mometrix.com/academy and enter code: 100340

Important Qualification

Not all anxiety is created equal. If your test anxiety is causing major issues in your life beyond the classroom or testing center, or if you are experiencing troubling physical symptoms related to your anxiety, it may be a sign of a serious physiological or psychological condition. If this sounds like your situation, we strongly encourage you to seek professional help.

Online Resources

Due to our efforts to try to keep this book to a manageable length, we've created a link that will give you access to all of your online resources:

mometrix.com/resources719/texesfcshnds

It's Your Moment, Let's Celebrate It!

Share your story @mometrixtestpreparation